Lost in the Fjord
The Adventures of
Two Icelandic Boys

by Jon Sveinsson

Translated by Konrad J. Heuvers

Illustrated by Irene Lin

Cover art by Frances T. Wilhelmsson

i

ISBN: 0-9886563-5-3
ISBN-13: 978-0-9886563-5-2

ACKNOWLEDGEMENTS

In this effort there have been many people to acknowledge. All of the great "Nonni friends" around the world who have kept his life and stories present for new generations to discover. The brilliant translation of Konrad J. Heuvers, the beautiful illustrations of Irene Lin, and the wonderful cover art of Frances T. Wilhelmsson (who knows what an Icelandic boy should look like because she has had a few of her own—including myself). Yet perhaps most of all we owe a debt of gratitude to Nonni's best friend who in her humility wishes to remain anonymous, yet without whom this project would never have seen the light of day.

CONTENTS

Lost in the Fjord

PUBLISHER'S FOREWORD

My father was born in a charming town in Iceland named "Akureyri." Such was his love for this place that he often spoke to me of it many decades after he had departed. We had planned to go to Iceland together in 2001, some fifty years after he had left, in order to see his beloved childhood home. However, he passed away suddenly just before we could. Thus I set out on my own pilgrimage to Iceland in order to honor my father's memory. I traveled all the way around that island nation at the top of the world and saw many beautiful and wondrous things. Yet when I arrived in Akureyri it had such a beauty and charm to it that I immediately understood all of my father's stories.

Little did I know that Akureyri would once again play a role in my life. For exactly a century ago a book was published in Germany about a little boy who lived in a charming town in Iceland named "Akureyri." His given name was "Jón Sveinsson" but his familiar name was "Nonni." And although he departed Akureyri at a rather young age, just like my father, he too had many stories to tell of his beloved childhood home. And later in life, after a career in ministry as a Jesuit priest, he did.

These stories would become so beloved that a community of persons known as "Nonni friends" would one day come together to celebrate and preserve them. Seeing my connections to both Iceland and Christianity one of Nonni's best friends reached out to me to tell me of her dream. A dream to produce an entirely new English edition of the most beloved of all Nonni stories in honor of the centennial of its original publication.

As I began to delve into this world of "Nonni friends" I soon came to see that the enduring nature of the Nonni stories is not without reason. For, in a certain sense, is it not a part of the human condition to forget one's parents warnings and become at times "lost in the fjord?" And, in a certain sense, do we not all have an innocent childlike nature somewhere within us that can lead us back onto the right course if we allow it to take the helm?

On this centennial of the publication of the original book, which was at the time dedicated to the centennial of the restoration of the Jesuit order, Chaos To Order Publishing is proud to present an entirely new English translation of one of the most beloved of all Nonni stories. May you and your loved ones through reading it soon become "Nonni friends" as well.

John C. Wilhelmsson

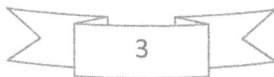

CHAOS TO ORDER
PUBLISHING
San Jose, CA
www.c2op.com

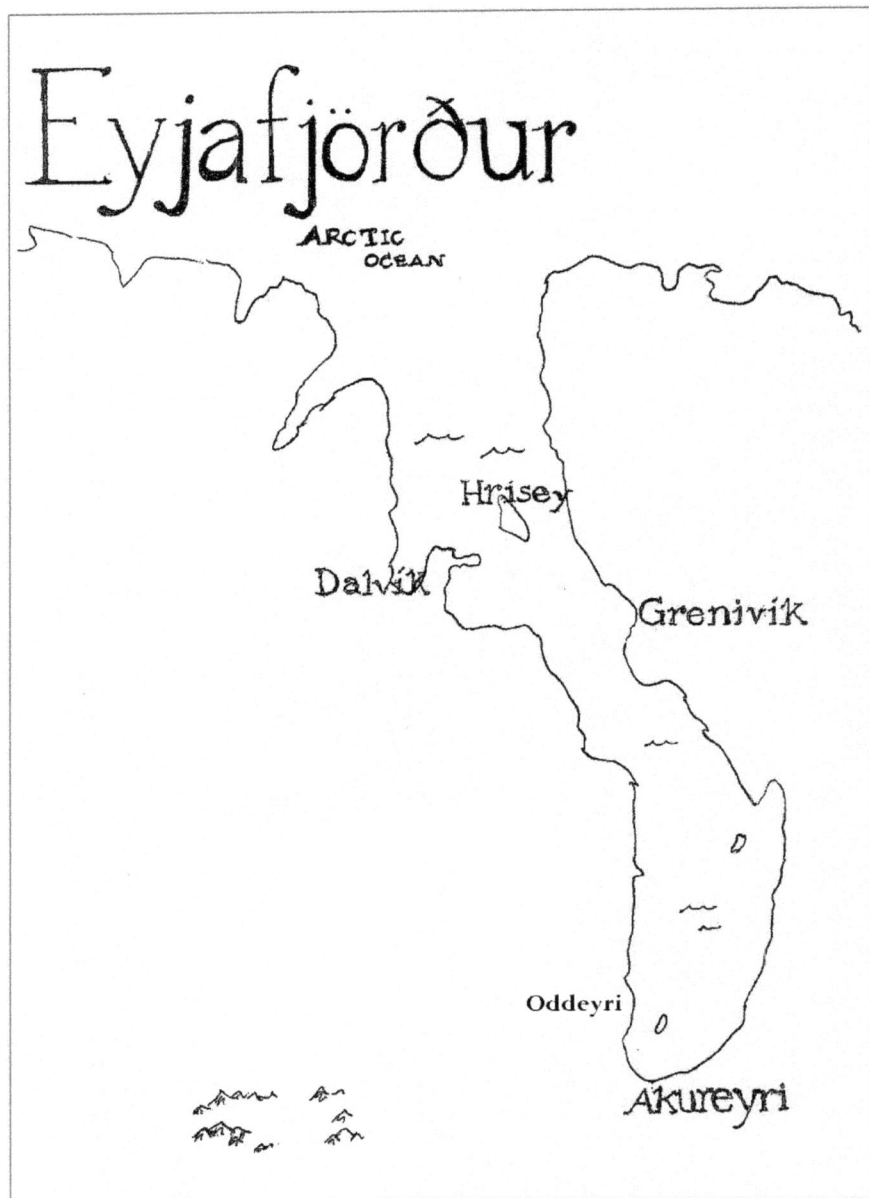

CHAPTER ONE

THE MAGIC FLUTE

At a time when I was an eleven year old boy and still lived in my home town, the charming little city of Akureyri, on the beautiful Eyjafjördur Fjord in northern Iceland, a man came to visit us. His name was Arngrim. He was distantly related to our family and was therefore especially well received.

Although his visit was nothing special it would have decisive consequences for the rest of my life.

After he had dined, Arngrim asked if he could play something on his flute.

"Oh yes" we unanimously answered.

I was especially curious because up to then I had never seen such an instrument.

Arngrim brought out a fine leather case, ceremoniously laid it on his lap, and opened it.

Then a superb polished black flute came into view.

It lay in several pieces there and had to be assembled.

After he took care of that, he placed the wonderful object on his mouth, wetted his lips, and began to play.

I was delighted. The lovely tones completely enchanted me. I didn't believe that I had ever heard anything so beautiful.

Moreover, Arngrim played masterfully.

Playing the flute was his passion. He said he never went on a trip without bringing his instrument.

Each time before playing he explained the sense of the following melody.

We heard different pieces from Germany, Denmark, France, and England.

Some of the melodies made such a deep impression on me that they still remain in my memory.

I became more and more enthused for this wonderful soft music.

This was my first exposure to musical expression.

In the evening, after everyone else had gone to bed, I slipped into our guest's room in order to beg him to teach me how to play the flute.

Arngrim was astonished at my youthful enthusiasm. He held my hands and said: "My little friend, I had not expected that. But unfortunately I can only stay here this one night. Therefore, there isn't enough time to teach you."

"Oh, I would try very hard. At least please teach me the basics tonight."

"Right now? You mean this evening when everyone else has already gone to bed? Do you believe that we would be able to do that?"

"Oh, yes we could do that. We could play very quietly."

Arngrim was amazed at my zeal and started to show me the basic principles.

I stayed with him unto late at night and practiced unceasingly.

Finally, I thought that I had learned enough from him and that I could learn the rest on my own.

Then I said:

"It appears to me that flutes make the most beautiful music that I have ever heard."

"You are right my young man. A certain secret magic lies in these notes. Even animals can not resist them. You can enchant snakes, rats, and even fish in the sea with them. In one German city there is the old story of 'The Rat Catcher of Hameln' (The Pied Piper of Hamelin). In it the flute player lures all the rats to come out and to follow him."

Entirely amazed I said:

"I can understand the rats. But, as you said, can one really attract fish in the sea with flute music?"

"Oh yes indeed my friend."

"Oh, then tell me how you can do that!"

"One must go to a lonely place on the ocean, lie there quietly, and begin to play. It is best to play long piercing notes and after that has been done for a while the fish will be lured to the surface. They will slowly swim around, listen to you and follow your boat wherever it goes."

"Is that possible? And do you believe that they will let me lure them?"

"Certainly my young man, if you play the right notes."

After all of this it had become very late. Therefore I had to hurry to bed.

That night I only dreamed of flute playing.

There are no rats or snakes on Iceland but there are lots of fish.

The ocean around there and the fjords teem with them.

My resolve was firm. I wanted to get a flute and lure the fish with it.

Shortly after Arngrim left on the next day I entered my father's office.

He sat at his desk.

Immediately I made my request:

"Father, I love playing the flute. Please give me money to buy one like Arngrim had."

He was surprised; he laid his pen down, turned around in his chair and said:

"So you want to buy a flute? Do you know that they are very expensive? I think that it would be better if we waited awhile. Later we could talk about this again."

"Oh father, I could buy a cheaper one. I would like to practice playing the flute so much."

My father smiled and said:

"Now, my young man, if you are so interested then you can go into the city and buy a little tin flute. You can have it charged to my account."

I thanked him and hurried to the city. A quarter of an hour later I had a cute little magic tin flute.

Every day I practiced with such zeal that soon I could play all the melodies known by me. I especially learned how to play long piercing notes.

If I had only known what fearsome suffering this "magic flute" would bring to me and my little brother just a few days later, then I would have thrown it at once into the fire.

But I didn't sense anything bad and went therefore happily and merrily toward the perils that lurked ahead for me.

CHAPTER TWO

AT THE HARBOR

One difficulty remained to be overcome. I had to get permission in order to go out on the big fjord.

In order to have companionship I went first to my younger brother Armann and said:

"Hey listen Manni (that was his nickname like Nonni is mine) would you like to go out on the fjord with me tomorrow in a row boat?"

"Oh sure, gladly. What do you want to do there?"

"Something very special. I want to play something for the fish on my flute."

"Wow! You want to play something for the fish on your flute? Do you think that they will be able to hear it?"

"Oh yes indeed, and you will see something very strange. I will lure the fish with it. But you mustn't say anything about this or else mother won't give us her permission."

Manni promised to keep silent. Then I went to mother and asked her to let us row out on the fjord to go fishing the next day.

Our mother granted her permission under the usual conditions that the weather had to be good and that we shouldn't get too far from the shore.

These conditions were not what I had in mind. I wanted to go farther from shore than usual. But I didn't say anything and just thanked her.

That was a mistake for which I would have to pay dearly.

The next day the weather was beautiful with sunshine and absolutely no wind.

The sky was blue and the air was saturated with the fragrance of countless numbers of wild flowers.

How happy Manni and I were! We could not have wished for better weather.

Very early we got everything ready.

We pushed our little red and green painted boat into the water.

I brought my fishing line with a little lead fish attached on the end. Two fish hooks hung out of its mouth.

As lures I temporarily tied red rags which the fish liked to bite on.

Just as I was helping my little brother climb into the boat an old woman came along. It was the widow Thordis.

Generally she was called the old "Vala." This

was a name the Vikings gave to their soothsayers.

Thordis was however not a soothsayer but was instead a good and pious old lady (I have changed some place names and personal names since many of the people mentioned are still alive).

"Where are you going children?" She asked.

"We want to go out on the fjord in order to go fishing."

Thordis saw the flute that was sticking out of my pocket.

"Are you also going to play the flute out there?"

I was somewhat embarrassed and said:

"Yes, just incidentally."

Thordis looked sharply at me and said:

"I don't know what will come from this. I am very worried about you two." Then she added slowly, "I hope that God will hold His protective hand over you."

These words made me feel uneasy. After a pause the old lady went on:

"Listen, Nonni, wouldn't it be better for you to give up this trip?"

"But why?" I asked.

Looking at my little brother she answered:

"It might go badly for you. It is dangerous for two little boys to go out alone on the fjord."

I started to have second thoughts and started to

think about giving up the trip. Then Manni called:

"But shouldn't we get started right away?"

"Yes," I answered involuntarily, "we should go now Manni."

I tried to conquer my fear and said to Thordis:

"We don't want to give up this trip. We are looking forward towards it so much and our parents gave us their permission."

"Alright, in God's name," said the old lady, "but at least don't go past the land spit, Oddeyri, and stay between the ships in the harbor. You have enough room there to play around."

I answered: "We'll be careful."

But I could not promise her to stay in the harbor between the ships. That would have defeated our plans. We needed to go further out and find a lonely place.

Therefore I broke off, said goodbye to the old lady and helped Manni into the boat. Then I sprang in myself and pushed off.

Manni cried out for joy as the boat slipped quietly over the mirror like and crystal clear water.

"Oh how beautiful, how beautiful!" he called out and clapped his hands.

I pushed a few times with an oar on the sandy bottom and soon we were out on the deep water.

Because Manni was still too small to row I said

to him:

"Listen, Manni, you are a clever young man. Today you should be the helmsman!"

He liked that. Right away he took his place.

I sat on my seat, grabbed the oars, and soon we were traveling rapidly over the silver shimmering water.

The rays of the sun glimmered like gold on the water.

In the distance foreign ships lay at anchor on the large harbor. They were washed by warm sunshine in the deep clear azure blue sea.

"Nonni," asked my little brother, "why don't we first row out to the ships and take a look at them?"

"Oh yes, Manni, I agreed. We have enough time. Let's steer over to them!"

There were about eighteen foreign ships out on the harbor.

Most of them were merchant ships from Copenhagen. Further out lay a whaling ship from Norway and a splendid luxury yacht from England. The owner was a rich Lord who was on an excursion to the interior of the island.

But the largest and most beautiful of all was "La Pandore," a French warship that was moored at the northern most position.

It had already been there several days and would

soon be ready to return to France.

There was a constant back and forth movement of small boats between the ships and land. So there was much for the two of us to see.

I rowed as fast as I could and Manni steered us towards the Danish ships that were moored nearest to it.

The first one that we came to was the one-masted "Rachel" from Copenhagen. It looked very graceful with its red painted railing.

We rowed around it and greeted the cabin boy who we knew. He friendlily returned our greeting and wished us a pleasant trip.

As we came upon the elegant well-built ship "Herta" the Danish sailors on board leaned on the railing and called out to us:

"Where are you going?"

"On a pleasure trip," I answered.

"Come up here to us," called out one of them.

"Thank you! But we are not allowed to go on board the ship."

"Who gave you that order?"

"Our Mother!"

"Why did she do that?"

"I don't know; I believe she was afraid that something might happen to us."

"What is she afraid of?"

"Once there was a little boy who went on a strange ship. It sailed away with him and no one heard anything more about him."

"That was a really horrible story. Just wait a moment; I will come right back." He disappeared in the ship's cabin.

Just to be careful we went a few meters away from the ship. "One can never know what he had in mind," I thought. But soon be reappeared and threw two large oranges into our boat.

"Those should quench your thirst," he called out.

I thanked him heartily and Manni blew him a kiss.

Then we rowed further and came upon the English luxury yacht. Its exterior was richly decorated with gold.

We rowed very close around it to carefully observe it.

While our boat slowly glided around the ship a few English faces looked at us over the railing.

The men wore red caps which we thought looked real funny.

They waved to us and called out some words to us of which we only understood:

"Good boys!"

We repeated the greeting and said "All right."

Those were the only English words that we knew.

The Englishmen laughed and called out again: "Good boys!" Once again we answered, "All right!" and continued our voyage of discovery.

One after the other we saw all the foreign ships and experienced many little adventures.

Finally the best came at the end.

We neared the powerful French steam screw frigate "La Pandore." We stayed there for a long time and looked at the warship with great wonder.

Also here the sailors gave us friendly greetings.

We saw lively young boys with sun burned faces and pitch black hair. They looked at us with the same curiosity for us that we had for them.

These were the little cadets who it is said were to become future officers in the French navy.

We waved to them and they answered us in French.

Unfortunately we didn't know a single word of it.

"Shouldn't we call back something to them?" asked my little brother.

"Yes, but we don't know any French." Manni made a suggestion:

"But at least you could call out 'Napoleon'" said the little rascal, "They would understand that!"

"Should I really do that Manni?"

"Oh yes do that. I am curious how they will respond."

Then I shouted loudly: "Napoleon!"

That made them enormously happy.

Ever more sailors and young boys appeared on deck.

They leaned over the railing and with smiling faces looked down on us two little Icelandic boys.

Manni radiated healthiness with his red cheeked round child's face. I, his older brother, was somewhat pale. Both of us had fair Icelandic hair and looked different to the darker Frenchmen.

"Manni," I now said, "it is definitely better if we row on because we are attracting way too much attention to ourselves."

"I also believe that," he repeated.

We waved goodbye and wanted to row past their nice rope stairway.

In this moment a steam launch from land came toward us and wanted to land where we were.

We hurried to get out of the way and make room for it. But after a call from the deck one of the occupants of the launch reached over to us with a long hook, fastened it onto our boat and pulled it.

Manni and I tried to get free and so there occurred a little struggle to the amusement of the observers above.

In due course we were overcome and were lifted out of our boat by powerful hands and placed at the foot of the rope stairs.

Here they let us wait for a while.

As we stood there and didn't know what was going to happen, I said to Manni:

"Now the French have captured us."

"It is so strange," he answered, "that they have seized us like this. Otherwise they seemed so good natured and friendly."

"Yes, they did that, and I believe that they only want to have some fun. In any case there is nothing for us to be afraid of."

In this moment an officer came over to us, and, in a friendly manner, took us by the hand and led us up above.

We offered no resistance because we soon noticed that they didn't want to do anything to us.

Up on deck we were received with the greatest politeness.

We saw everywhere only friendly faces and to our right and left everyone reached out their hand.

The officer led us now a long way over the

roomy deck, past the shining polished cannons, and past the stern sentries marching back and forth with their drawn shining sabers.

We climbed down a set of steps and came to a door made of the finest mahogany. It led into a gorgeous little parlor.

Everything here was exceptionally fine and neat.

The officer invited us to sit at a table that stood in the middle. He brought out a beautiful picture book from a cabinet on the wall and laid it out in front of us.

Through signs he let us understand that we could look at it and then he left the room.

While we were alone I said to Manni:

"Marvelous! It is happening to us here exactly as we have often read in 'A Thousand and One Nights.'"

Manni answered:

"Yes indeed and it seems to me that they are treating us even better than the princes in the stories."

"That is true, Manni. But what do you think they plan for us?"

"I don't know," said Manni, "perhaps they want to take us with them to France, like the Turks once took many Icelanders to Algeria."

I had to laugh at this silly idea and said:

"That wouldn't happen! You must know all the Icelanders that the Turks captured were enslaved. It seems to me that the French are treating us much better than they would if they planned to take us away as slaves."

"That is true, Nonni. I wouldn't want to go to France as a slave but would certainly enjoy traveling to that country."

"Oh Manni, that would be a fine thing."

At that time we didn't know how soon this wish would be fulfilled!

We then began to turn pages in the picture book.

It wasn't long before the door was opened and a man wearing snow white clothes entered. It was the pastry cook for the warship.

He greeted us friendlily and placed a pair of plates with cakes and other delicious things on the table. Then he filled two little glasses with white wine and invited us with a gesture to take them and then left.

"The French are amiable people," said Manni.

"Oh yes that is indeed true," I added.

We began to eat. The cakes and the sweet wine significantly raised our cheerful mood.

We were finished and the officer entered.

We went right over to him, reached out our

hands to him, and said according to the custom of our country:

"Thank you for the refreshments!"

He appeared to understand what these words meant, squeezed each of our hands, and led us out.

We followed him over the deck and went to the forward part of the ship.

Here we were led into a bright room.

A gentleman with a photo apparatus was waiting for us. He straightened up our clothing and put us into a suitable pose. I had to sit on a stool and my little brother on the other hand had to stand on my right side and lay his hand on my shoulder.

So we were photographed and the gentleman thanked us with a broad smile and a small bow.

Then we went out on the deck again and met a large number of little cadets who in their French vivacity tried to speak with us.

But we couldn't understand anything that they said. Except for calling out "Napoleon," I was not able to begin a conversation.

The lively young French boys accompanied us down the stairs to our boat. Here they filled our pockets with cookies and raisins.

Then we gave cordial farewells to each other. With all good wishes for a blessed future.

CHAPTER THREE

OUT FISHING

Under constant gesturing and waving of hats we slowly departed from the magnificent "La Pandore."

We saw that everyone was looking at us so we tried to maneuver our boat as perfectly as we possibly could.

The eight year old Manni sat confidently at the helm like an experienced seaman. For my part I handled the oars as perfectly as possible.

Once we were far enough away from the ship I started to row with all my might and traveled over the velvety smooth water with such speed that snow white foam splashed up at the prow.

After I got tired rowing, I pulled the oars up in the air and let the boat glide along by itself.

It was delightful to slip along like that on the still water.

"How do you like our trip?" I asked my little brother.

"Oh, very much! But that was especially nice by the French!"

"Oh, yes and now we know what they intended. They only wanted to take pictures of us."

"This way they will at least have our photos to take back with them to France. After all they couldn't take us there personally."

"Yes," said Manni, "that was certainly all that they wanted. But I must say their cakes really tasted good."

"Oh, let's not be too greedy Manni. We should rather try to catch some fish!"

"Good. But we have to first find a suitable place."

"We have that right here Manni. We can stop and throw out the lead fish lures with the hooks."

We had already gone far out into the fjord and we had traveled a long way from the harbor where the foreign ships were anchored.

In our thoughtlessness we forgot the admonishments that both our parents and old Thordis had given us.

I drew the oars into the boat and said to my brother:

"I propose that we stay here until we have caught a fish for everyone in our household: one for father, one for mother, one for our sister, one for the servant girl, and one for each of us. That would be six of them. Afterwards we will row further north until we reach the tip of the land spit Oddeyri where I will try to enchant the fish with my flute."

"Good," said Manni, "let's do that!"

I took out the lead fish lure and threw it into the water.

"Oh, couldn't I be the first one to catch a fish?" asked my little brother.

"Yes you can do that if it would make you happy. But that one must be for our mother and you know that her favorite fish is plaice (a type of flounder)."

"Good," said Manni, "then I will catch a plaice."

The lead fish lure quickly sank, ever deeper and deeper, until it reached the bottom of the sea.

I handed Manni the fishing line, he wound it around his hand he pulled it up a foot because he knew that plaices liked that depth.

Then he watched and waited like a lynx.

Meanwhile I took some of the French cakes out of my pocket. They really tasted good. Then Manni called out:

"A plaice has bitten!"

"Then pull the line up!"

He began to do that but soon called out:

"Oh no! He slipped off. He isn't there now."

"That's okay Manni, don't worry. There are lots of fish here. Let your line out again and you will see that right away you will get another bite."

Indeed, the little lead fish hadn't sunk to the

bottom yet and he called out:

"Nonni, I have already caught another one."

"This time, Manni, it can't be a plaice. The little lead fish didn't go down deep enough. You have certainly caught a cod. Is it big?"

"No, it seems to be rather small because I only feel a weak tugging on the line."

"That's too bad! Just pull it up quickly!"

Manni did that and soon pulled a little flapping cod over the edge of the boat and let him fall beside the rowing bench.

"Look how funny he is!" he called out after he looked at the fish carefully "He has a black spot on his nose."

I carefully removed the lead lure out of the fish's mouth. The hook had caught on the corner of its mouth through its lower lip.

"Hey Manni, why don't we let this poor fish go. It is too young and small. After all you wanted to catch a plaice and not a cod."

"Yes," he said. "That would bring us luck."

I threw the fish into the water and instantly he shot like an arrow into the deep.

Once again Manni lowered the lead fish with the two hooks down to the bottom. After just two minutes he called out:

"I have already caught another one!"

He pulled it up.

This time it was actually a plaice with gorgeous round purple-red specks on its back.

"This one is for mother!" he said as he took the flapping fish from the hook and laid it in the boat.

"Now you can catch the other remaining five, Nonni!"

"I would be very happy to do that," I said and let the lead fish lure sink to the bottom.

Then I pulled it up a few yards because I only wanted to catch cod and those are mostly found at that depth. Soon I felt a constant yanking and pulling. It must be teeming with fish down there.

They constantly nibbled on the hooks without making a firm bite.

But it didn't take long until I felt a strong pull on the line.

"Now I have a big cod," I cried out, and quickly pulled the line up.

Manni eagerly watched.

"Oh, no! Look Nonni," he called out as I pulled my catch out of the water. "You have caught two fish at the same time!"

Indeed there were two cod hanging on my double hooked lure. One was big and one was smaller.

First I laid the big one next to the plaice. It was

almost two feet long.

As I started to release the smaller one from the hook I was involuntarily startled. He had the same black spot on his nose like the one we had just thrown back into the water.

I was even more astounded when I discovered that he was wounded in the corner of his mouth.

He was in fact exactly the same fish that had been caught before. Also Manni was astonished and said:

"That is indeed unusual! This time we should keep him, Nonni."

"Good, then he is for you, and the bigger one is for father."

I continued fishing and in less than ten minutes had caught the remaining three fish that we wanted.

Now I took the oars in my hands again. Manni sat at the helm and we made a rapid trip towards the north.

When we reached the tip of the land spit Oddeyri, I raised the oars and rested, because I was completely covered with sweat. The boat floated gently on the deep water. Everything was still and silent.

But this was a very dangerous position.

At the ebb tide the water rushed with great force out of the fjord into the open sea. On the other hand at the flood tide the current from the sea to the land was so strong that the water flowed high up on the shore.

On the other side of the land spit the fjord widened significantly and much further north was the open Atlantic Ocean.

It was for that reason that our father and mother had strictly forbidden us to row north of the dangerous land spit Oddeyri.

We had not planned to do that but we had come very close to that precarious position.

In our youthful thoughtlessness we were so wrapped up with our plans to play the flute and to lure the fish that we didn't think about anything else.

I took out my flute and said to Manni:

"Now pay attention. Look into the water and search for the fish while I play. See if they come up to the surface."

"Oh, yes, yes, Nonni. Start playing!"

He leaned over the side of the boat while I played the prettiest tunes that I knew.

We were very eager and attentive. The smallest ripple and the slightest movement on the water surface caused us great excitement.

At any moment we expected to see fish sticking their heads out of the water.

But we didn't see anything, didn't hear anything, and didn't think of anything other than the fish who were supposed to be lured by the music.

However, they disappointed our expectations and remained below in the deep sea.

"It is strange how long this is taking!" said Manni at last.

I was also losing my patience.

Could Arngrim have misled me? Oh, no that was impossible! He had told me that I must be patient even if it took a long time for the fish to come up.

I should persevere and not give up hope yet.

CHAPTER FOUR

IN GREAT DANGER OF DEATH

While we played the flute and watched the water we two unfortunate young boys didn't notice that the sky had become over clouded. The weather had become damp and cold. Fog had come down between us and the land. It became thicker and thicker and enshrouded everything around us in an impenetrable sinister dusk. But what was even worse, we didn't notice that the ebb tide had begun and a strong current had grabbed our boat and pulled it out past the land spit Oddeyri.

We were on a quick trip toward the long wide part of the fjord and the open sea!

Manni was the first of us to notice our danger.

"Nonni!" he called out, "what has happened! I can't see the land anymore!"

"How can that be? What do you mean you can't see the land anymore?" I replied horrified as I looked all around us.

In fact I saw nothing else except impenetrable grey fog.

"Oh my God!" I called out. "Now we are lost!"

I threw my flute in the boat and grabbed the oars in desperate fear.

"Manni, steer us to the city!"

He jumped at once to his helm position but then gave me a questioning look and said:

"But where is the city? I don't know where to steer the boat."

I looked around to try to get oriented. But that was all in vain. I didn't have the slightest idea where South, North, East, or West was.

I thought about our situation and was convinced that the ebb tide had already driven us too far out. Now in the east and the west we wouldn't find any sandy beaches. There would likely only be steep rocks that jutted perpendicularly out of the water.

Thus it would be impossible for us to make land fall even if we succeeded in reaching the coast. What could I do now? The city lay way off to the south. But we were being swept away from it on a rapid voyage.

We were in great danger of death.

Manni sat at the helm and looked at me with tears in his eyes.

I was the leader and was supposed to determine what to do.

Finally I said to him:

"Manni, isn't there some way that you can determine in which direction south lies?"

He looked to the right and then to the left and then pondered. Finally he shook his head and said:

"Nonni, it is impossible to find it."

"Then God must help us because I am completely lost."

For a while we sat there in silence staring out at the impenetrable fog that continued to get ever thicker.

Then I took the oars in my hands again and said:

"I will at least do what I can and hope by good chance to row in the right direction."

For a long time I rowed with all my strength.

The boat slipped quickly over the calm and smooth surface.

But where were we going? We couldn't tell.

Were we traveling towards the rocks in the west or the east? Or were we rowing against the current toward the city? But in this case we were staying at the same spot, because it was impossible to overcome the strength of the current. Might I be rowing due north? In that case we would be traveling with the flowing current and I would be speeding up our down fall.

I pulled up the oars again, went over to Manni, and sat next to him.

For a long time we sat quietly next to each other. Then Manni said:

"Why aren't you rowing anymore?"

"Because it won't help us. I don't know where we should row and you know it even less than I do."

Manni was quiet.

"It is horrible!" he said, after a long pause.

"You are right," I answered.

Yes, our situation was horrible.

We sat next to each other and without speaking looked at the fish that lay in the bottom of the boat in front of us.

After a long time Manni looked at me. His eyes were full of tears.

"Poor Manni!" I said and pressed both of his hands tenderly.

To me it felt like he was freezing.

"Oh, dear Manni, you are freezing. Your hands are so cold and you look so pale. Is there something wrong with you?"

"Oh, it isn't that bad Nonni. But it is true that I am very cold."

"Poor brother, I am so sorry that I can't help you!"

"It will soon pass, Nonni."

Alas, I knew that was not the case and that this was only the start of our suffering.

But I kept these thoughts to myself and took care not to say anything about them.

The dampness and the cold continued to worsen and it continued to get dark.

Was night approaching or was the fog getting thicker?

We didn't know the answer because we had no idea of how late it was.

I pressed Manni close in order to help give him some warmth.

I loved my little brother so much and didn't want to see him suffer.

He laid his head on my breast and closed his eyes. We sat like that for a long time.

I looked at him. Oh, he was not getting better.

His face which normally radiated good health was becoming paler and paler.

How I blamed myself for my carelessness! It was my fault that he was suffering.

Finally he opened his eyes and asked:

"Can't you see any land at all?"

"No, Manni, we are being driven steadily out into the long wide part of the fjord toward the open sea."

Then he said:

"Oh, how cold it is! I wanted to go to sleep but couldn't because of the cold."

Each word cut into my heart. But what could I do?

I didn't have any sort of cover to wrap him up in.

Then I remembered that we had the cakes and raisins in our pockets. They might help us. They wouldn't warm us but would keep us from being hungry.

Therefore I asked Manni:

"Are you hungry?"

"Oh, yes, but I am suffering more from the cold."

I suggested that we eat our cakes and raisins. He happily agreed and he ate almost all of them.

That helped somewhat. We felt a little refreshed and strengthened. But we were still cold.

I was also very cold.

I felt Manni's hands again. They were icy cold and his face was pale as a corpse.

I was terrified. I had to do something to help him.

Then I had an excellent idea. I was wearing a fairly warm jacket.

I quickly stood up and took it off.

"Manni," I said, "come, I will help you put on my jacket."

"Oh, no, Nonni, I can't do that. You will get ill without your jacket."

"Don't be afraid! I am much older than you and can stand more. Come put on my jacket!"

"Oh, Nonni, I don't believe you can stand the cold without your jacket. Please keep it for yourself."

"What do you mean? I can stand that. Don't you remember last year when I was buried for several hours under the snow on my way from Akureyri to Hals? That was much worse than now."

"Yes, but you did become ill from that."

"Certainly, but it only took me one night to recover. I was fully recovered on the following day."

Finally he gave up.

I put my jacket on him over his thin blouse and buttoned it up.

Then we crouched together on the seat at the helm position and hugged each other tightly.

We tried to sleep and lay there with closed eyes.

After a long time I looked at the little one. He looked better to me.

The warm jacket had definitely helped him. That made me so happy that I almost forgot how cold I was.

Although Manni lay there with closed eyes, he appeared to still be awake.

"Are you sleeping," I whispered to him.

He opened his eyes and shook his head. Then he sat up and said:

"Do you know what just came to my mind?"

"No, what could that be?"

"I believe that the reason we can't fall asleep is that we haven't said our evening prayers. Our mother says that you fall asleep quicker and sleep more peacefully after saying your prayers. Shouldn't we do that Nonni?"

"Oh yes, lets pray together!"

We knelt down and each of us said the usual evening prayers that we prayed at home.

After we were done, I asked him to recite one of the pious children's verses that our mother had recently taught him and that I had not memorized.

He was ready to do that and recited the following Icelandic prayer (which follows in an English translation):

"Oh my Jesus,
Let one of your hands
Be my bed,
And the other my cover.
Then no harm will befall me.
Oh, Jesus, friend of children
Let me never be separated from you.
And if I should die,
Take my soul
Into your hand
And carry it into paradise.
Oh my Jesus,
Let your dear and
Purest angels
Stand by over our bed
On this dark night.
May they watch over us
And keep us from harm
For under their watchful protection
We are safe from all danger."

We finished with an "Our Father."

Then we sat down next to each other and embraced each other.

"Don't you think that it will be better now," asked Manni.

"Oh, yes, I think so."

"And do you believe that God will hear our prayers?"

"Certainly, Manni."

"Mother says," continued Manni, "that God always hears us if we pray with devotion and trust. Isn't it true that we have done that? Now, Nonni, we don't need to be afraid any more. God and his angels are now with us."

Although I was accustomed to such childish words from my little brother, now they made such a special impression on me that tears ran down my cheeks.

Manni continued:

"So, Nonni, now we can lie down again and will certainly fall asleep. And God will certainly rescue us from this danger."

Instead of answering him, I was deeply moved and hugged the little one tightly.

My little brother was a truly pious and innocent boy and was therefore loved and respected by all who were close to him.

Now he was a true guardian angel for me. Because of him we had said our prayers and childish words out of his innocent heart had so deeply moved me that my despondency was turned into confidence.

We snuggled together again, holding each other tightly and actually fell into a deep sleep.

So we lay there, enveloped in fog, guarded by good angels, and rested carefree on deep water in a frail boat that the powerful current of the Eyjafjödur was driving out toward the open sea.

CHAPTER FIVE

AMONG THE WHALES

I don't know how long our sleep lasted but it was interrupted in a very surprising manner.

Namely, we were awakened by being suddenly thrown from our seat onto the bottom of our boat.

As we came to our senses we heard an unusual swishing and rumbling around us.

At the same time a stream of pelting rain fell down on our boat

The ocean was disturbed and our boat was being tossed around by the waves.

But the strangest thing of all was that there was no wind blowing and that the pelting rain stopped just as quickly as it had started.

We wanted to stand up, but after our long sleep and the cold night we could scarcely move at first.

After we succeeded in standing up we fell down right away.

The boat rocked so much that we had to kneel and firmly hold onto the rowing bench.

The strange swishing and rumbling and the peculiar splashing of the water near us was so powerful that we both involuntarily cried out.

We couldn't understand what could be wrong.

The thick fog took from us any sight and made our position so scary.

Paralyzed with fright we didn't say anything at first.

Finally Manni began to speak:

"But where do these waves come from Nonni? There is no sign of wind here!"

"Yes, Manni, that is also a mystery to me."

"And where is the rain coming from? A moment ago it was really pouring and now it has suddenly stopped."

"I can't explain it," I answered him and looked out at the water that was wildly churning around us.

These were not the quiet broad ground swells that sometimes occur in calm weather. These waves were of a different type, irregular and foaming.

"What can be making the water move like that?" asked Manni again, as he snuggled up to me in fear.

"I believe," I answered him, "it is a large ship that is traveling past us right now or perhaps it is an earthquake."

I had scarcely spoken these words than a wave lifted our boat higher in the air than before. This happened so suddenly and without any recognizable reason that we became even more distressed. We looked in the direction from which the waves were coming.

Then a sight came to our eyes that filled us with horror.

We saw right next to us, only a few yards away, a powerful pitch black glistening monster breaking the surface of the ocean.

At the same time we heard that peculiar rumbling from before and at the same moment we saw something that looked like a thick white column of smoke that rose perpendicularly up in the air, coming out of the monster.

What had looked like smoke to us fell like rain into the sea and a portion onto us.

Now all of the phenomena were clear to me. We were heading into the middle of a school of whales that were cavorting on the surface and squirting large jets of sea water up into the air.

I recognized at once the terrible danger in which we found ourselves, because the huge whales would not even notice little boats like ours.

If it should happen that a whale surfaced out of the water directly under us then our little boat would be picked up on its powerful back like a nut shell, hurled up into the air, and certainly be capsized.

Thus, as fast as possible we had to find a way to escape from this terribly dangerous place.

Without delay I put both oars into the water and asked Manni to steer us away from the whale that swam next to us on the surface.

I rowed with all my strength and quickly moved the boat away from that dangerous position.

Just then I saw the animal suddenly raise the huge front part of its body up in the air and then slowly dive into the sea.

While doing this its hindquarters came a little out of the water and after lashing its tail to the right and left it disappeared into the ocean depths.

Through strenuous rowing we were soon away from the school of whales.

Here the water surface was again quiet.

Never the less I continued to row for a while in order to get as far away as possible from the dangerous monsters.

Finally I pulled up the oars and sat down next to my brother.

Although the adventure with the whales had really upset us we didn't talk anymore about it. We were too worn out and uncomfortable.

"What time could it be" asked Manni.

"I think about midnight."

"I believe it is much later," he said, "certainly two or three o'clock."

He could indeed be right; we had slept for a long time.

I was again worried about him because he still seemed to be suffering. I suggested that he sit in the middle of boat on the bench and row a little to get some exercise.

He did that right away.

"But you must only use one oar," I said to him, "because you are too little to use both of them."

He was able to do that while I used the other oar to steer the boat and keep it moving.

After a few minutes Manni said:

"That was good advice. Now I feel better."

"Let's keep doing this," he added.

Suddenly he pulled up his legs and called out in alarm:

"What is going on? Water is running into the boat!"

I instantly sprang up and bent over to take a look.

Yes indeed, the water was streaming in from the bottom of the boat.

The water had already risen up to the floor boards over the keel and we saw that it continued to rise!

I went down on my knees and pulled up some of the floor boards in order to find the hole where the water was coming in from.

The hole had to be quickly plugged or the boat would soon be filled with water which would result in our certain death.

I put my right arm into the water and looked for the round hole that is always located on the bottom of the keel of Icelandic boats and is closed with a wooden plug. After a trip, when a boat is pulled up on the beach, the plug is removed so that any water which has seeped in can run out.

I thought that perhaps this plug had come out.

That is what happened. The little hole was open.

"Manni," I cried, "the wooden plug is gone, look for it quickly!"

"Where can I find it?"

"It must be floating in the water somewhere in the boat."

Manni kneeled on the rowing bench and looked everywhere for it.

But the plug was nowhere to be found.

While he was looking I had tightly pressed my hand against the hole, but I couldn't stop all the water from coming in.

A cold shiver ran through my body.

I was completely soaked since I was kneeling in deep water.

"For God's sake, Manni, hurry, I cannot stop the water, it is going to go over my shoulder."

"I can't find the plug! It is nowhere to be seen."

The situation was desperate!

Suddenly I had a good idea:

"Take your knife," I called, "and cut off my shirt sleeve!"

Manni followed my command, cut off the sleeve, pulled it down and gave it to me in my left hand.

I wadded it together and pressed it firmly into the dangerous hole.

Now I could get up.

But the boat was now half filled with water.

We looked for the bailing scoop.

Unfortunately we had forgotten to bring it and there was no time to lose.

We had to get the water out of our boat as soon as possible. Otherwise wind or waves might come that could quickly fill our little boat with water.

We stood there helplessly.

Finally Manni cried out:

"We could use our caps to bail out the boat."

"Excellent idea! That will work!"

Without delay we started to work. But the bailing took a long time.

Finally we emptied the boat.

Now we finally found the missing wooden plug; it had gotten stuck in the bottom of the keel.

I quickly put it into its proper place; then I put on the wet shirt sleeve and tied it on with a piece of fishing line.

Happily we had overcome this great danger and now we could sit down again at our place next to each other at the rear of the boat.

But soon we experienced what it means to spend a cold night sitting in an open boat totally wet and soaked to our skins.

"If only God would soon help us!" I sighed.

"He will certainly do that," answered Manni, "we have prayed for that."

"But, Manni, it is really bad for us."

"That is true, but mother says, God tests us when He doesn't help us right away."

"Dear, Manni, if only God doesn't test us too long! I feel so miserable."

"Oh poor Nonni, your whole body is soaking wet and you don't have a jacket. I will give you yours back."

"No, no, I won't accept it."

I had to vigorously argue to convince him to keep the jacket.

He then tried to comfort me by saying that he was sure that help would soon come.

In the meantime it got much worse for us. We continued to freeze and all the members of our bodies were getting stiff.

"Shouldn't we pray an 'Our Father' together?" said Manni, "then God will come to our help quicker."

We prayed an "Our Father."

Then we sat there quietly and waited.

Lost in the Fjord

CHAPTER SIX

THE VOW

We must have looked like shipwreck survivors the way that we sat there huddled together, pale, weak, and completely soaking wet. Moreover, there I was in mere shirt sleeves of which one was temporarily tied on with fishing line.

We were both so completely miserable. We couldn't go on like this much longer.

We had to get help soon or else it would be over for us.

After a long pause Manni said:

"How are you Nonni?"

"I feel very weak. I am sure it is the same for you."

"Yes, I almost feel as if I was going to pass out. But, Nonni, a thought came to me. Seamen in danger like us are often said to make a vow to God for His help in rescuing them. Shouldn't we also do that? Then perhaps He will be quicker to help us."

"That is a good idea. But what vow should we make?"

Manni answered:

"You must remember the story that our mother read to us about Francis Xavier the great missionary to India."

"Oh yes, Manni, I remember it well."

Although we were Protestants our mother had a book at home about the life of St. Francis Xavier which told us about his missionary activities in India and Japan.

Furthermore, just recently she had told us about St. Peter's church in Rome. Our Savior lives in it and He listens to all the good people that come to visit it.

She also told us that in the Middle Ages many Icelanders made pilgrimages to Rome. At that time all Iceland was Catholic.

These stories had made a great impression on both of us.

Manni remembered that right now. Therefore he said:

"Don't you remember what a saintly man Francis Xavier was?"

"Oh certainly," I answered.

"Do you know what we can do Nonni? Why don't we make a vow to God that when we grow up we will also work for him and convert the heathens exactly like Francis Xavier?"

Manni's proposal made me hesitate. To me the vow seemed to be somewhat presumptuous. Yet I accepted it and said:

"That is a very serious and important vow but I will gladly make it with you."

"Let's do it right now Nonni. Otherwise it might be too late."

We gathered our thoughts for a moment and then vowed to God that we would emulate St. Francis Xavier if He would rescue us from our danger.

When we were finished we both looked all around to see if His help would immediately come.

But there was nothing to be seen.

We sat on the rowing bench again. I noticed that Manni's condition had worsened.

He looked like he was close to death.

I pressed him close to me and put my arms around him.

He closed his eyes, leaned his head on my chest and stopped moving.

That lasted for a long time.

A shiver ran through my body!

Had my brother passed out? Or was he sleeping? Or was he perhaps dying?

"Almighty one, dear God; Oh help us! Help us!" I repeated without a break.

Suddenly, to my great relief, Manni began to move, but without opening his eyes.

Several times he lifted his hands up and called out with a smile on his pale face: "Jesus, my Jesus!"

At once I guessed that he was having a dream because he often talked in his sleep. Therefore, I was careful not to wake him.

Anyway he soon woke by himself, rubbed his eyes, and looked around in bewilderment.

It was as if he had been far away and couldn't at first determine where he was.

I gently stroked him on the cheek and helped him to wake up. Then I spoke to him:

"Dear Manni, you slept so quietly! That was certainly good for you."

"Yes, Nonni, but I am sorry that I woke up so quickly!"

"I believe that and can think of a reason for that."

"What do you mean Nonni?"

"Because you repeatedly called out: Jesus. You must have had a nice dream."

He gave me a serious and astonished look and a subtle red flush came over his face. Then he said:

"Did I really call that out?"

"Yes, Manni, you smiled and raised your arms in the air as if you were speaking with someone.

Won't you tell me about your dream?"

He was embarrassed. But then he answered:

"Yes, I would be happy to do that; it happened so quickly; because it was very short."

Then he told me the following:

"As soon as we had made our vow I fell asleep.

It seemed to me as if the saintly missionary Francis Xavier floated down from heaven. He took me by the hand and I floated with him through the air far, far away from here.

We came to a big city which had a very beautiful church.

After my question about the name of the city, he answered it is Rome and the large church was St. Peter's cathedral.

Next he led me through a big door into the church.

There I saw Jesus.

He stood at the high altar.

At once I ran up to him. He came toward me, spread out his arms and looked kindly at me.

I met him in the middle of the church.

He embraced me there.

At that moment I woke up."

Manni's story moved me and I called out:

"Oh what a beautiful dream!"

"Yes, it was beautiful," replied Manni, "and I cannot tell you how happy I felt in the arms of Jesus! I was completely out of myself in happiness."

"I understand that my dear little brother! Jesus seems to love you very much."

"Yes, I believe that also," he answered in all simplicity, "and I am completely sure that he will send us help soon."

CHAPTER SEVEN

ON THE FRENCH WARSHIP "LA PANDORE"

Suddenly, while we were talking, we thought that we heard a muffled wailing sound.

"Do you hear that Manni?"

"Yes, I distinctly heard it. What could it be?"

"I don't know what it is," I answered.

In the greatest suspense we sat there and listened.

It was not long before we heard the same sound again.

We looked at each other in amazement but neither one of us had an idea of what it could be.

We were all ears; then the long drawn out wailing sound came again and came ever nearer.

Suddenly it came to me in a flash: "That is a ship Manni, which is coming through the fog towards us!"

"A ship! But what is that sound?" "That must be a fog horn."

"Then we are saved!" called out Manni full of joy. "Let us quickly thank God; because it was through Him that this help has come!"

So we folded our hands and thanked God from the bottom of our hearts for the help that was now approaching us.

After saying our thanksgiving prayers I said:

"Now we have to make one last great effort to row toward the ship. Otherwise, it could pass us in this thick fog."

We noted the exact direction from which the signal came and rowed, as much as my weakening strength allowed, toward the rescuing ship.

Soon we saw a black mass that was very slowly gliding along toward us.

"That looks like a mountain!" said Manni.

It was the hull of a ship that in the fog looked much bigger than it actually was.

Now it was necessary to attract the attention of the sailors, especially the seaman who was on watch.

I did my best in order to get as close as possible to the steam ship.

"Manni," I cried, "quickly pick up my flute, which lies behind me, and blow on it as loud as you can."

Manni grabbed it and blew. At the same time I shouted out at the top of my voice: "Help! Help!"

Nothing was to be seen of the man on watch.

"That is strange," I thought, "he would usually stand forward near the bowsprit."

I suddenly saw him but only for a moment.

Oh no, he was looking at the other side and then his line of sight was blocked by the high railing, because our boat came too close to his ship!

As we came next to the ship we recognized it again, it was "La Pandore," the French warship that we had visited the preceding day!

The large ship had thus left the harbor in Akureyri in the morning and was now on its way back to France.

"That is a remarkable coincidence!" said my little brother.

We were now only two yards from the side of the steamer.

"Didn't anyone see us?" asked Manni.

"I don't think so. At least I didn't see any sign of that."

For us this was a matter of life and death.

The engine made such a noise that Manni's flute playing and my cries were completely drowned out.

I cried out in mortal fear:

"Oh no, what if the ship steams off without noticing us?

At first we were at the forward part of the ship and now it was indeed gliding past us without anyone answering our calls for help.

Then at the place where the stairway was lowered, I discovered a thin rope that was hanging down from the railing and was dragging in the water. Instantly and quickly I stroked with the oars right next to the ship where the rope was hanging.

I grabbed it and held onto it firmly. Quick as lightning I wrapped it around my wrist and at the same time threw myself under the backmost rowing bench so that I would not be pulled into the sea. Fortunately the bench was tightly nailed.

At first the rope did not tighten but instead just glided for a while over the railing.

Then it became taut.

I cried out in pain because the jerk was so strong that I thought my hand would be torn off.

Our boat was lifted up in the air by its bow and now traveled along as fast as the ship.

In spite of his weakness Manni came over to help me. Then with our combined effort we succeeded in wrapping the thin rope once around the rowing bench and tightly tying it.

We were fortunate that the steamer was going so slow because of the fog. Otherwise, it would have been impossible to grab the rope and to fasten it.

"Nonni," called my brother suddenly, "we have lost an oar. See, it is floating away in the water."

Unfortunately that was true.

During our desperate work with the rope it had fallen overboard and disappeared in the wake of the steamer.

Nothing could be done about it.

Now that we had firmly tied up the boat we called for help again.

But this was all in vain. The noise of the churning water from the ships propeller overwhelmed all other sounds.

Out of weariness we finally had to stop shouting.

"What are we going to do now?" asked my brother.

"See there Nonni," he said then, "just above us is a porthole. Perhaps you can reach it with our one remaining oar?"

I looked up and noticed the little round window.

"That is an excellent idea Manni! I am surprised that I didn't see it."

I tried to reach up to the window with the oar.

It worked. Immediately I began tapping on the thick disk of glass.

"This will work better than all our shouting," I said.

And indeed, after a few minutes Manni cried:

"Look! Someone is at the window!"

It opened and a sun burnt face with a pair of vivacious black eyes appeared in the round opening.

"Ahoy!" I called, "help us!"

Instead of answering, the Frenchman gave us an amazed look.

Of course he hadn't understood anything that I had shouted.

After he had looked at us for a moment he pulled his head back and closed the little window.

We were now in great suspense about what was going to happen.

After the passage of a few minutes a head appeared up above over the railing.

It was the same one that had looked out of the window.

Soon others were also visible and before long there was a crowd there.

The people looked down on us in astonishment.

We noticed that they were speaking with each other and eagerly gesticulating. But because of the noise of the engine and the propeller we couldn't hear anything.

"If only they would come quickly to help us," said Manni. "I am horribly cold."

"Take comfort Manni," I replied. "They will certainly not make us wait long. Once we are up there you will see how good they will treat us. Just think about how friendly they were yesterday!"

"Do you think that they will give us dry clothes?"

"Without doubt they will. And not only that: they will lay us in warm beds and offer us something to strengthen us. And then we will quickly recover our strength."

"If I could only get warm that is all that I need," said Manni.

All at once while we were talking we heard a loud clanking over our heads.

We looked up and saw that a section of the railing had been pushed aside.

"Now they are certainly going to lower the large stairway," said Manni.

And soon they let it down on the side of the ship. After a few minutes everything was ready.

An officer and two strong sailors climbed down and pulled our boat close to the lowest tread of the steps.

The two sailors had large woolen blankets under their arms and jumped into our boat.

The one grabbed Manni right away and placed him on the rowing bench.

The other one wrapped him in the blanket, took him under his arm, and climbed up with his burden.

The first one now wanted to do the same thing to me but I was ashamed to be treated like a small child in front of all these people. I slipped past him and jumped without his help, but with great effort, onto the step.

I must have looked very miserable as I stood there in my shirt sleeves, soaking wet, pale, and shivering from the cold.

They didn't let me go any farther, but instead wrapped me up in a blanket and carried me up the steps.

Up on the deck a great number of officers, sailors, and cadets were gathered.

Instead of the cheerfulness with which we were received the day before we now saw worried and even shocked faces.

They took us to the after deck. The officer led the way and the sailors carrying us followed him. A broad staircase with shiny brass rails on both sides led down a dozen steps to a very nice little cabin with two bunk beds, one on top of the other.

The officer pulled open the purple red curtains.

Both bunks were made up with snow white linen sheets and blue woolen blankets.

A polished mahogany table stood in the middle of the cabin. On each side of the beautiful room there were blue velvet covered sofas by the wall.

After a sign from the officer the sailors laid us down, wrapped up as we were, on the soft cushions of the blue sofas.

I stood up right away and sat down next to Manni.

Meanwhile the officer gave the sailors some orders.

Although we didn't understand anything he said, we noticed they were talking about us, because he pointed his finger at Manni and then at me.

The sailors gave us a friendly nod and left the room. Now only the officer was with us.

First he took Manni's pulse and then also mine.

"He must be a doctor," whispered my little brother.

"I believe you have made the right guess. We are now safe. We are in good hands."

"I also believe that," said Manni. "Do you see how well our dear God has helped us?"

"Yes," I answered, "that is wonderful. But we have also made an important vow to Him. Do you believe that we will be able to keep it?"

"God will certainly help us keep it, Nonni."

We couldn't speak anymore because there was a quiet tap on our door.

"Come in!" called out the doctor, and two French boys came in. They looked about my age.

I was amazed at how considerate they were.

They must have thought that we were much worse off than we actually were, because they looked so serious and walked on tip toes so as not to make any noise.

One of them carried a white basin with warm water and the other one carried a bundle. In it was new underwear for us.

From the sofa I held out my hand and nodded friendlily to them.

They repeated my greeting in the same way and appeared to be happy that we were not as afflicted as they had thought.

Then the doctor came over.

The agile boys helped us to take off our wet shoes and socks and to wash our hands and feet.

After we had put on the dry clothes, we were hurriedly tucked into bed. Manni was put into the bottom bunk and I was put into the top bunk.

While we were being carefully covered up Manni called up to me:

"Now we are certainly sailing to France."

"Yes Manni, but we can't do anything to change that, so we shouldn't worry about it."

After the doctor had made sure that we were warm and comfortably tucked into bed he brought each of us a glass of a warm good tasting drink.

This drink was like a ray of sunshine to us. A pleasant feeling of warmth and wellbeing streamed throughout all the members of our bodies and soon we fell into a refreshing sleep.

We must have slept for a long time, certainly for most of a day, but finally we were awakened by a loud noise that penetrated into our little hospital room.

The sound came from the engine. It whistled and hissed as if it had gone berserk.

It seemed as if the ship wanted to stop.

I opened my eyes and looked around.

The first sight that met my eyes was a French boy sitting at the table and reading a book.

I sat up in my cot.

At once the boy sprang up and looked at me in a friendly manner.

"Oh, can't you tell me how late it is?" I asked him.

Instead of answering, he smiled, laid his hand on my chest and gently pushed me down.

Then he said something to me that sounded just like Chinese and very carefully covered me up again.

Now it was clear to me where I was and what the situation was.

We tried to converse with each other. But neither one of us was able to understand the other.

Finally we shook our heads, looked at each other, and both of us started to laugh.

That woke up my brother. Suddenly I heard his voice from the lower bunk.

"Nonni, how are you?"

"I feel completely refreshed Manni. But I am so hungry."

"I also feel the same."

My little brother rose up and sat at the edge of his bed so he could look up at me.

But our hospital orderly did not approve of that. He pushed him back into his bed.

"Nonni," called out my brother, who was not accustomed to such strong constraint, "the boy is holding me tight and isn't letting me rise up."

"Then I will come to you," I answered him.

I was just about to get up. But the French boy held me back.

"Non! Non!" he called out and forced me to remain laying there.

All of my resistance was to no avail.

"Non! Non!" he repeated again.

"Manni, he won't let me come to you either and keeps on saying 'Non! Non!' to me. It is strange how he mispronounces my name."

"At the same time," said Manni, "he pronounces it so oddly through his nose."

I tried to make it clear to the little French boy that my name was Nonni and not Non.

But he didn't understand me.

The good boy gave us a sad look.

Certainly the doctor must have given him orders to be sure to keep us lying in bed. He had not believed that we would be so lively.

But we calmed him down soon by staying in our bunks.

After a long pause Manni called out.

"If only they would give us something to eat!"

"Then tell that to the French boy," I answered him.

"That won't help because he won't understand me."

"That's alright, then I will make myself understood to him through signs."

I waved to the boy and tried to use signs to show him that we were hungry.

To my great joy I saw that he had understood me. He gave me a friendly nod and went out.

Shortly after that he came back with the doctor.

We greeted the distinguished gentleman with vigorous handshakes to let him know that we were healthy and lively.

He examined us and was very happy with our condition.

Then he spoke a few words with the boy who quickly left. But then he came back with our clothes.

While we were sleeping they had been washed and dried.

Now we were allowed to get up.

As we prepared to take off the borrowed underwear the doctor made signs to us that we were to keep them.

We were deeply moved by this friendliness and then gave him a hearty handshake to thank him.

We had scarcely finished washing and getting dressed and then the white dressed ship's cook entered. This time he didn't just have wine and cakes but instead a full noontime dinner.

The table was set for four.

The two French boys were allowed to eat with us. That meant the hospital orderly and the other one who had been so helpful to us.

Before these two sat down at the table they made a sign of the cross and devoutly prayed a short grace.

This edified Manni and me and we tried to copy it as much as we could.

During the meal all four of us were lively and conversed with each other. The two French boys spoke French and the two of us spoke Icelandic.

After the first two courses my brother and I were full.

We had properly helped ourselves and didn't expect anymore.

But they treated us like princes and kept on bringing us more food.

We were not accustomed to such elegant meals so we contented ourselves with sampling each of the fine dishes for the sake of companionship.

On the other hand for our two friends it was a different matter. They were accustomed to such large noon time dinners and understood them better than us.

They urged us to eat and appeared to regret that we had done so little justice to such a spectacular meal.

After we were finished we stood up again and said a prayer to thank God for the meal.

"These Catholics are really pious!" my brother whispered in my ear.

Then we went up on the deck.

Now we experienced a great surprise. The warship had indeed stopped and lay motionless on the still sea.

Not far from us was another ship.

It looked very nice but was significantly smaller than "La Pandore."

A Danish flag flew from its sternpost.

"That is the "Fylla!" called out Manni, after he had a good look at the strange ship, "isn't that true Nonni?"

Now I could clearly see it and to my great happiness recognized that Manni was right.

It was indeed the Danish warship "Fylla" that occasionally visited Akureyri in the summer.

It was certainly on the way there now and could bring us home.

"It is almost a miracle," said Manni, "the way God has looked after us."

"Oh yes, I say that too," I answered.

But we couldn't converse anymore because the crew of the "La Pandore" had gathered around us. All of them wanted us to know about their interest in us.

At first we were a little bashful, but the French sailors, especially the little cadets, were so friendly to us that our shyness soon disappeared.

All around us they reached out their hands. We squeezed them with inner thankfulness.

The radiant sunshine that was shining from the beautiful evening sky was reflected on all the faces.

At the boarding steps the captain was already waiting for us.

He was a powerful older gentleman of noble appearance with a kindly, almost paternal, face.

"I believe that we must thank him for their hospitality," I said to Manni.

"Yes, we will do that," he answered.

Somewhat shyly we approached the distinguished gentleman.

Kindly he smiled down on us.

Full of thankfulness I grabbed his right hand, squeezed and shook it heartily and thanked him in my Icelandic language for the rescue and for all the good things that we had enjoyed on his ship.

"Manni," I said, "you must also thank him."

He grabbed the left hand of the captain and placed a kiss on it in his child like way.

The captain now laid his left hand on Manni's head and his right hand on my head and friendlily stroked our hair.

The large powerful man was visibly moved. There was a tear in his eye.

Then I thought that perhaps he remembered his own boys back home.

Before we went down the steps we turned around one more time and said farewell to everyone.

Everyone all together answered with warm words that we could not understand.

Then we climbed down.

Below there awaited us not only our little boat but also a splendid steam launch from the warship.

We were completely bewildered by such a great honor.

Our dear doctor and the two boys who had helped us were already sitting in the launch. The French flag flew on the staff behind them. We sat next to the doctor.

Some sailors climbed in and firmly tied our boat to the launch.

Quickly we left the splendid "La Pandore" and sailed to the "Fylla."

Once again we turned around and lively waved our caps.

For the last time the Frenchmen waved farewell to us and quickly we sailed over the mirror like sea.

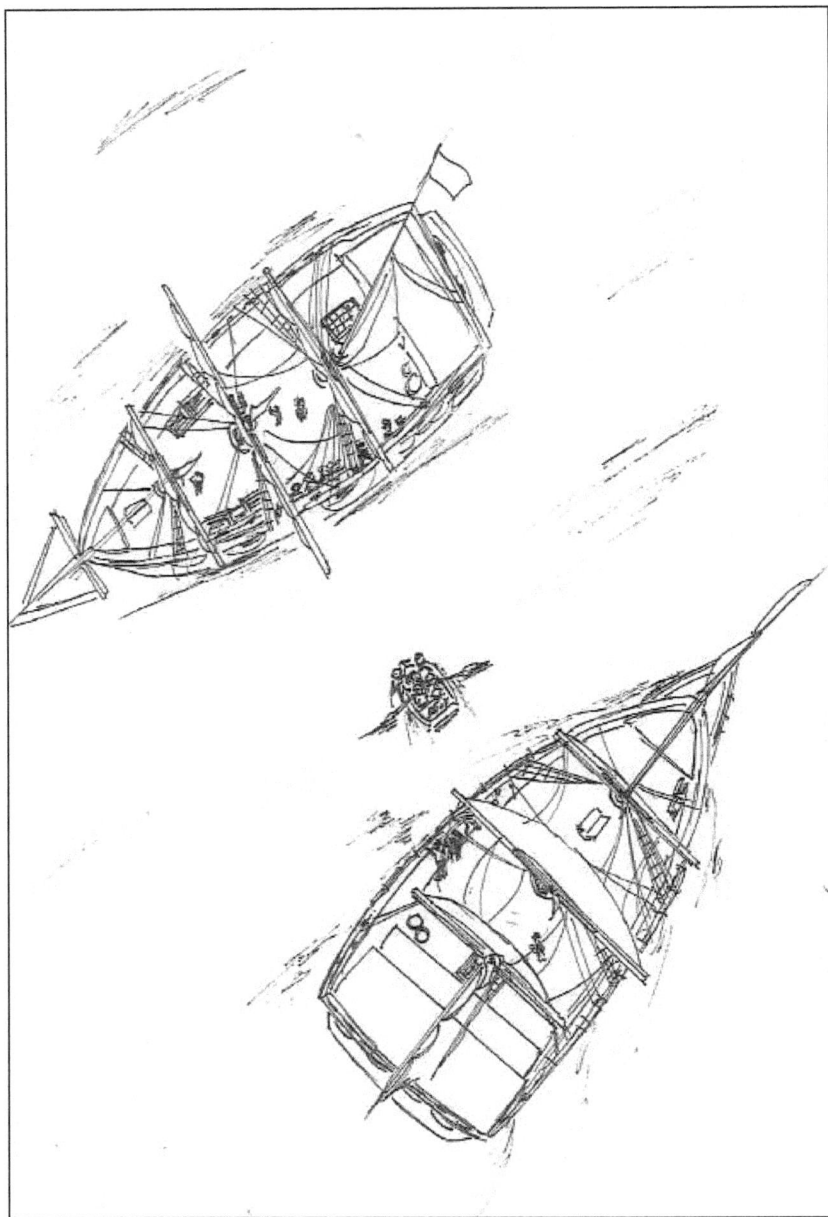

CHAPTER EIGHT

ON THE DANISH WARSHIP "FYLLA"

For a long time our visit on the proud French warship was a pleasant memory. In fact we have never forgotten that visit.

On the way to the Danish ship the sun offered a magnificent view to us.

It was an incredibly beautiful summer evening.

The thick fog and cold of the previous night had vanished without a trace.

The sun had stopped in wonderful brilliance on the horizon. Up here in the summer it shines throughout the night.

The sharp bright light of the daytime sun has now gradually changed into the mild shimmering midnight sun.

It was a mixture of rose and purple that spread out a gold red shine over everything.

A wonderful path, shining in the colors of the rainbow, formed on the surface of the ocean and spread out from our launch off in the distance toward the splendid midnight sun.

This golden pathway was gorgeous beyond all measure. It shined, sparkled, and glittered in constant motion.

It looked like it was strewn with millions of pearls and jewels.

It was an enchanting sight.

Now we arrived at the boarding steps of the "Fylla."

We were received by two Danish officers in magnificent uniforms.

The French doctor, the two cadets, Manni, and I were led up to the deck. However, the sailors remained in the launch.

The Danish seamen greeted us in their typical comfortable and caring way.

They looked at us with a certain curiosity while we moved over the deck to the captain's cabin.

The doctor together with the officers led the way and we four boys followed unobtrusively behind them.

We noticed right away how tidy and clean everything was on that beautiful ship.

The deck was scrubbed white and washed so that not a speck was to be seen.

The canons and all the metal ware shined as if they had just been polished.

We walked down the elegant cabin steps and met the captain. His drawing room was just as elegant as any that we had seen on the French ship.

The captain of the "Fylla" was a distinguished and gracious gentleman with a black moustache and a short cut hair. He went over to the French doctor, grasped his hand and shook it heartily.

Then he asked him to sit on the velvet upholstered easy chair.

Then he came over to us boys, shook our hands, and pointed out a red cushioned bench against the wall where we could sit.

The two gentlemen spoke French with each other.

Naturally Manni and I didn't understand a word of it. However, the two little French boys followed the conversation with visible interest.

We were well aware of what they were talking about. It was certainly our adventures that were being communicated by the doctor to the captain because the gentlemen as well as the two boys all looked up and smiled at us.

"It is annoying," whispered Manni to me, "that we can't understand any of that. I believe they are talking about us the whole time."

"That is certainly true," I answered him, "but just be still; they are certainly not saying anything bad!"

Just then there was a knock on the door and a young cabin boy entered.

He carried a tray upon which there was a bottle of champagne, six glasses, and a silver dish with pastries.

He set it on the table and with a ceremonial gesture removed the cork from the bottle, filled two glasses with the sparkling wine and then he glanced inquiringly at his master.

The gracious captain looked at the doctor and pointed at us four boys who sat quietly and modestly on the bench.

The doctor smiled and with a gesture of his hand appeared to give permission for us to be given a helping of that fine wine.

We also understood this language.

With beaming faces we looked at each other as the captain took the bottle and filled our glasses.

But one of the glasses was only filled up half way as he gave a fatherly glance at Manni.

We were asked to come closer.

We took our glasses and clinked them with those of the distinguished gentlemen.

After Manni had drunk his mouthful of champagne he said softly to me that the wine was good and he would have liked to have had a full glass. But he was satisfied with what he got.

Then the visit came to an end.

Manni and I gave a warm farewell to the Frenchmen.

The doctor gave us friendly pats on the head and we thanked him sincerely for all his kindness.

We exchanged several warm handshakes with the boys and then we ran down the boarding steps, sprang onto the launch and said goodbye to the sailors who had waited for the doctor and the cadets.

Soon the launch went back to "La Pandore" with much waving and motioning from everyone.

Soon after that the two warships moved off.

The French ship steamed out toward the Atlantic Ocean and the Danish ship steamed toward Akureyri.

It would be difficult to describe in detail how well my brother and I were treated on the Danish ship.

Overall we encountered the same courtesy and friendliness that we had received from the French.

In addition there was the fact that we could understand some Danish and were able to make ourselves understood to them.

Everyone who knows the Danes knows how courteous and friendly they are to deal with.

They also did all they could to make our visit on the "Fylla" as pleasant as possible.

People took us around and showed us the sights on this warship.

In the officer's mess an officer took two little elegant swords and put them on us. We were allowed to wear them while we were on board.

There were three Danish boys on the ship.

Naturally we immediately made friends with them and found them to be a lot of fun to play with.

In the evening we ate with them.

During the meal Manni asked how it was arranged that the two ships stopped on the sea. He thought that at such a great distance it would not be possible for them to communicate.

The boys answered that mariners had signal flags which allows them to communicate with each other. Doing this is called "signaling."

The French ship, they continued to explain, had signaled to the "Fylla" the following message: "We have two Icelandic boys on board that we have just fished out of the Eyjafjödur. They live in Akureyri. Would you be willing to take the two boys home?"

The "Fylla" answered right away: "Yes."

We knew the rest of the story.

Then the boys asked us to tell them something about our adventures.

We told them about our fishing, the fog and the current, about the whales and the horrible night out there, about our vow, and about our miraculous rescue.

When we told them about the whales they said that on the same morning they had encountered a school of whales.

They had squirted a vast quantity of water into the air and to the great delight of their crew they had played about.

Two them had swum along the side of their ship and suddenly dived into the sea.

"These must have been the same ones that squirted us with water," said Manni.

But the boys could not understand how the whales could have squirted us with water.

They thought that it must have been foam from a wave.

This conversation was so engrossing for all of us that we sat together in the purple red rays of the midnight sun until it got quite late.

Finally, we went to bed. Manni and I shared a cabin with the Danish boys.

We soon fell to sleep. And even though on the "La Pandore" we had already slept most of the day, now on the "Fylla," we fell asleep again and didn't wake until the sun was high in the sky.

When we woke we noticed right away that we were already in the harbor of Akureyri. The engine had stopped working and everything was still and quiet.

We quickly got dressed and ran up on deck.

If we were not mistaken, the "Fylla" lay at anchor almost in the same place that "La Pandore" had been.

The cheerful sailors circled us, wished us luck, and joked around with us.

Our friends, the little boys, now came to us and led us to the officers' mess where we and they had breakfast together.

We received the favorite Danish dish: a warm rice pudding, sprinkled with sugar and cinnamon, and a piece of butter in the middle.

After breakfast we went below to visit the captain in his cabin.

He greeted us friendlily and pointed at our little swords. He smiled and asked if we had decided to join the Danish navy as cadets.

We answered that we would have to first ask for our parents' permission.

"That is nice of you," he said and then told us the following:

"Already early this morning, when we first arrived, a boat from land came to us and asked about you."

That news made our eyes open wide.

"Yes," he continued, "your parents were in great fear since you disappeared and quite a few boats were sent out to look for you. Fortunately I was able to give good news about you to your father and mother. I let them know that you are on board in the best of health and that I will bring you home as soon as possible."

Both of us stood up, gave the good captain our hand and thanked him for everything he had done for us.

"Oh, dear children, you don't have to thank me," he answered, "but to calm your parents it would be best if you went home right away."

But he added to this: "As long as the 'Fylla' lies at anchor here, you are welcome to come on board to visit whenever your parents give you permission."

Completely delighted over his friendliness we heartily thanked him.

Then he personally took us up on the deck in order to be present for our departure.

A snow white launch had been lowered into the water, our little boat was firmly tied to it, and three sailors received orders to row us to land.

We returned our little swords and gave the entire crew a warm farewell.

The three boys, that we had come to like so much, were already standing on the boarding steps and waiting for us.

When Manni saw them he had an excellent idea and ran to the captain and said:

"Oh, please captain, may the boys come with us?"

The captain laughed and gave the requested permission.

"But you must be responsible," he turned to Manni, "that they come back and don't stay away like you!"

"I will do that captain," answered Manni.

Then he ran down to the three boys and told them that they were allowed to go on shore with us.

They were very happy about that, because ordinarily they almost never get permission to go on shore.

Lost in the Fjord

CHAPTER NINE

HOME AGAIN

Once everything was ready for our departure we climbed into the launch.

From the water we shouted to the Danes a last farewell and they answered "Paa Gensyn" (Danish for "Until we meet again").

"In which direction should we row?" the sailors asked me.

Before I could answer Manni already shouted: "May I steer? I certainly know the right direction."

"Very gladly," answered the sailors and gave him the helm right away.

So with a certain pride Manni took command of the beautiful launch.

But the little rascal didn't steer us directly to our house but instead sailed past some of the foreign ships.

They were still anchored in the same places they had been two days ago.

As is the usual custom in small towns, so it is in Akureyri. The report about our disappearance had spread everywhere both in the city and at the harbor.

Therefore as we passed the foreign ships they knew us right away and asked all sorts of questions.

But we didn't give any details and instead only gave short evasive answers:

We stated that we had been out fishing and had become a little lost. That is the reason that we had returned on the warship "Fylla."

They laughed and shook their fingers at us.

Some of them even predicted what a discomforting reception we might expect at home and through descriptive hand movements made it clear what could be in store for us from our parents.

We didn't like that so Manni gave the sailors a signal to keep on rowing and steered us in a straight line to our house.

This lay rather near to the beach next to the church.

When we reached the shore we sprang onto the land and asked the sailors to pull up the boat on the dry sand and to leave it there for the time being. Because, by all means, they and the boys that came with us should come with us to meet our parents.

They accepted our invitation, pulled the boat out of the water, and went with us.

At our home they had seen us coming and the door was already open even before we reached the entrance.

Father, mother, and our oldest sister Bogga received us with the greatest warmth and for the time being there was no hint of any unpleasantness for us two sinners.

We were after all the two "sons" who had been thought dead and now returned home again alive, fresh, and lively.

That joyous event had to be celebrated.

Therefore our companions were invited to a cup of coffee with cake.

While we happily and cheerfully sat at the round table in our parlor the sailors and the little Danish boys insisted on telling everything that they knew about our adventures.

After they had presented their report to our great relief they asked our parents to not punish us, because all the suffering that we had endured was sufficient punishment for the mistakes that we had made in our inexperience. They humbly requested that we not receive any further punishment.

They added that we had behaved exemplarily on the warship.

This request from our visiting guests could not be refused by our parents.

So we had more reason to thank these good people.

Instead of punishment we received full forgiveness.

Then I told my mother how kind the Danish boys had been to us.

To show them her thankfulness she got a box of raisins and divided it up among them. They didn't turn down the little gift and after visiting us for an hour they left our house.

Manni and I accompanied them to the beach where we especially thanked the sailors for pleading with our parents for us.

When they were departing and we shook the hands of the boys we were so sad that tears came to our eyes.

The launch sailed off and we went home.

Already on the afternoon of that same day I felt certain unease because of the vow that we had made out on the sea. And I asked myself the serious question: "How can we keep what we have solemnly pledged to God?"

I decided to talk with Manni about this before evening.

Therefore I looked for him and asked him to go for a stroll with me.

He was ready to go right then and we went up the high heather covered hills near the city.

There we sat down on a rock that stuck up out of the flowering heather.

For a while we sat there without talking and watched the harbor with the foreign ships. The "Fylla" was the largest of all of them.

Then I interrupted the silence and said to my brother:

"Manni, what do you think about the vow which we have made? That is a serious matter. Because, when you make a vow to God you have to keep it."

"Certainly we have to do that" he answered. "God has helped us so wonderfully."

"Yes, but we have vowed to imitate St. Francis Xavier and like him win souls for God. How can we do this? He was a Catholic and a Jesuit as well. We can't become Catholics and certainly can't become Jesuits."

Manni looked at me with his wide open innocent eyes and said:

"I also don't know how that will happen. But I trust that the Savior will help. He can do anything and we have to leave it to Him."

This was always Manni's answer when he had to face a dilemma.

He was a God loving soul and left the solution to all his difficulties to the Savior.

I replied to him:

"What you have said is all good but then in the mean time we must ask God for help and never forget what we have vowed to Him."

The little one said he agreed with that and we went home in a cheerful mood.

Lost in the Fjord

NONNI AND MANNI

EPILOGUE

Through the concurrence of different circumstances, or properly said, through divine providence, just a year later I unexpectedly received an invitation to travel to France in order to complete my studies there at a Jesuit boarding school.

Three years later my brother followed me there.

We were Protestants like all of our countrymen and had the customary prejudices against the Catholic church and even more so against the Jesuits.

Yet after we became acquainted with the Catholic Church and learned more about it we decided to join it.

Concerning the Jesuits, we treasured them as thorough and loving teachers. We came to admire them so much that at the end of our high school studies we entered the order.

We never regretted those two steps.

Manni, who always remained the same good and pious boy, died in 1885 while he studied philosophy in Louvain five years after joining the Society of Jesus.

Unfortunately, it was not possible for me to be with my dear brother at his death bed.

I had already returned up north and lived in Copenhagen.

My pain at his death escapes description.

For my mother words cannot express her sorrow at the news of the decease of her darling.

Characteristic, however, of her and her maternal love is the following that will surely strike a deep resonance and inner understanding in the heart of any mother and any child who reads these lines.

I had to report the death of my brother to her in a letter.

She wrote me back at once and tried to comfort me in my sorrow and to affectionately console me without saying one word about her own pain.

I knew my mother and knew what that meant.

In the following years we omitted (as if in consequence of a silent agreement) to mention our dear Manni, so as not to enlarge the constantly bleeding wound in our hearts.

Twenty years later in 1905 when I lived at our Gymnasium in Ordrupshöj near Copenhagen she wrote me the following noteworthy lines:

"My dear Nonni!

For the first time today I was able to read to the end the letter that you wrote me twenty years ago about the death of my dear Manni.

As I opened it and then noted what it concerned, I was not able to read any more. I had to fold it up and leave it undisturbed until now."

Five years later my aged mother followed her darling into eternity. And so I stand alone now like a stranger among my fellow men.

With my little Manni and my dear mother were taken from me the greatest natural comfort of my life. I have never known a greater earthly love as that for them.

Only the hope to see them again in another world comforts me.

And concerning Manni, the comforting and trusting idea comes to me, that at the end of his earthly journey, as he lay in his last struggle in Louvain, he was secure in the embrace of our Savior just as in that dream vision when he was a small child in that night on the deep waters of the Eyjafjörður.

CHAOS TO ORDER
PUBLISHING
San Jose, California
www.c2op.com

ABOUT THE AUTHOR

This thrilling story "Lost in the Fjord" was written by the famous Icelandic author of children's books and Jesuit Jón Sveinsson* (up to now the only Icelandic Jesuit). He was born on November 16, 1857, at the farmstead Möðruvellir in North Iceland. When he was a boy his nickname was "Nonni" and that is why the 12 books about his adventures and experiences are called the "Nonni books". During the twentieth century readers of all ages throughout the world devoured the stories of his adventures and the Nonni books became bestsellers – published in approximately 40 languages.

This is a new translation into English of the original German title "Nonni und Manni" which was written over one hundred years ago. It describes a dramatic event in the lives of two young Icelandic brothers. The action occurs in the Eyjafjördur Fjord in North Iceland - the homeland of the two boys. This event played a significant and life changing role in their future lives.

Before Jón Sveinsson became a writer he traveled throughout Europe giving many talks about his adventures in his fascinating Icelandic motherland – the country of ice and fire. Children and grown-ups filled large lecture halls and listened breathlessly to the charismatic Icelander. With his white beard and kind blue eyes the tall man himself was an impressive figure who caught everyone's attention. He loved children and they loved him in return. They even sent him letters begging to be taken along on his journeys. His readers could scarcely wait for his next book to appear.

May this book's trip through the United States, Canada, and other English speaking countries be as successful as Nonni's first visit to the "new world" in 1936 when Jón Sveinsson arrived in New York by steamship. This was the first stop of his trip around the world at the age of 80 years instead of taking 80 days as in Jules Verne's famous science fiction story!

On his North American trip he was a guest of Fordham University for three months. He then traveled to Winnipeg where he visited his youngest brother Friðrik and other Icelandic immigrants to Canada from Akureyri that he knew before he left Iceland as a 12-year-old boy in the autumn of 1870. The last stop in North America was San Francisco where he had been invited to stay at the university. After two months Nonni continued his world trip and traveled across the Pacific Ocean on a Japanese steamship to visit Sophia University in Tokyo for a year. There he was the guest of Fr. Hermann

Heuvers S.J., the second president of the university. In 1938 Nonni returned to Europe via China, the Indian Ocean, the Red Sea, through the Suez Canal on to Gibraltar, and finally back to London. After resting from the long journey Jón Sveinsson started to write two very interesting and fascinating books in German about his trip around the world, namely "Nonni in Amerika," and "Nonni in Japan." He finished writing the first one but unfortunately could only complete 39 chapters of "Nonni in Japan" before his departure on his last trip - to heaven. His lifelong friend Hermann Krose added the chapters 40 – 44 after studying Nonni's detailed diaries and Herder published the books posthumously. Nonni died peacefully on October 16, 1944 at the age of 87 in Cologne, Germany, and was buried there in the Melaten Cemetery.

The author's Icelandic name is "Jón Sveinsson" but he changed it to "Svensson" once he started writing his books in German. He feared that his German readers might mispronounce his surname. Thus his "nom de plume" has become "Svensson" except in Iceland.

Lost in the Fjord

THE ORIGINAL GERMAN VERSION

The first publication of the German language version of "Nonni und Manni" was in the Jesuit Calendar for the Jubilee Year 1914 which celebrated the centennial of the restoration of the Jesuit order on Aug.7, 1814. It was so enthusiastically received that it was also printed in book form in 1914 (see Appendix). It is not surprising that there was a need for a second edition in 1915.

According to the World Catalog there are both 1914 and 1915 editions of "Nonni und Manni". We also have an undated edition with 86 pages (which is the length of the undated 1914 edition) and our undated 2nd edition also has 86 pages. Both of our undated editions have identical Publisher's Forewords. We also have a dated third edition which appeared in 1918 which has 127 pages. It has a slightly different Publisher's Foreword and an Author's Preface. Thus, our 2nd edition must have appeared in 1915.

In 1918 there was such a demand for the book that two editions were published. This shows that "Nonni und Manni" was a very popular book in German speaking countries.

APPENDIX:

Information about the original German version of the book.

Translation of the Title Page of the 1915 Edition.

Nonni and Manni. Two Icelandic Boys

by Jón Svensson

with illustrations by Fritz Bergen

Second Edition

Regensburg

Josef Habbel Publisher

PUBLISHER'S 1915 FOREWORD

This story received great acclamation upon its first appearance in the Jesuit Calendar for the Jubilee Year 1914.

The lively description of an experience which was to be significant for the future development of two Icelandic boys could not fail to make a deep impression.

But there is something else. Due to its content and its concept the story is of a high instructional value. To an exceptional degree it has the potential to be an instructive, supportive, and nurturing influence on our youth. It offers them a shining example of deep brotherly love and true religiosity.

After deliberations and after encouragement by experienced directors of educational institutions and academies the publisher decided to produce the story in book form.

May this story find much appeal and create rich benefits!

The Publisher

ABOUT THE TRANSLATOR

Konrad J. Heuvers was a world renown Mathematician and the nephew of Fr. Hermann Heuvers S.J. Fr. Heuvers was a Jesuit missionary and the President of Sophia University in Tokyo during Nonni's visit to Japan in 1937-1938. He was Nonni's host during the visit and is mentioned in several chapters of Nonni's last book, "Nonni in Japan" which was recently published for the first time in English by Chaos To Order Publishing.

A Journey Across Iceland

The Ministry of
Rev. Jon Svensson S.J.

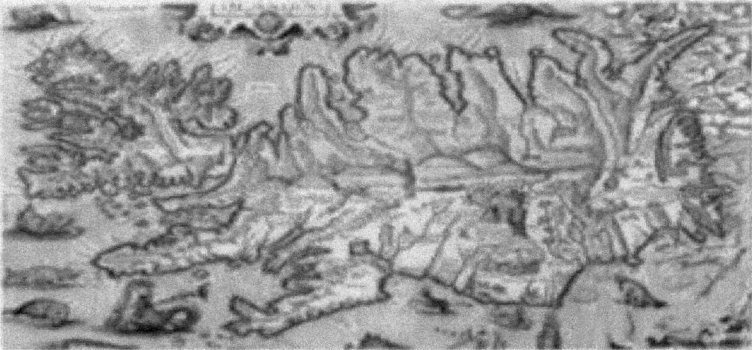

Revised and edited by
John C. Wilhelmsson

A JOURNEY ACROSS ICELAND

The Ministry of Rev. Jon Sveinsson S. J.

by Jon Sveinsson

Edited by John C. Wilhelmsson

Jon Sveinsson (or "Nonni") is the only Jesuit priest ever born in Iceland. He left his homeland as a boy, with his beloved brother Armann (or "Manni"), to follow their mutual call to become Jesuit missionaries. Although Manni has since passed on during his studies, Nonni is now the Reverend Jon Sveinsson S. J. The boys had wished to become Jesuit missionaries, like St. Francis Xavier, yet Jon Sveinsson has spent most of his time in the order so far as either a student, and now an instructor, in academia. Still longing to fulfill his dream of becoming a missionary he has volunteered to travel to Iceland to care for the souls of his fellow countrymen. Such is the premise of this classic Icelandic travelogue written by the man who would later became one of the most beloved children's authors of all time (large print).

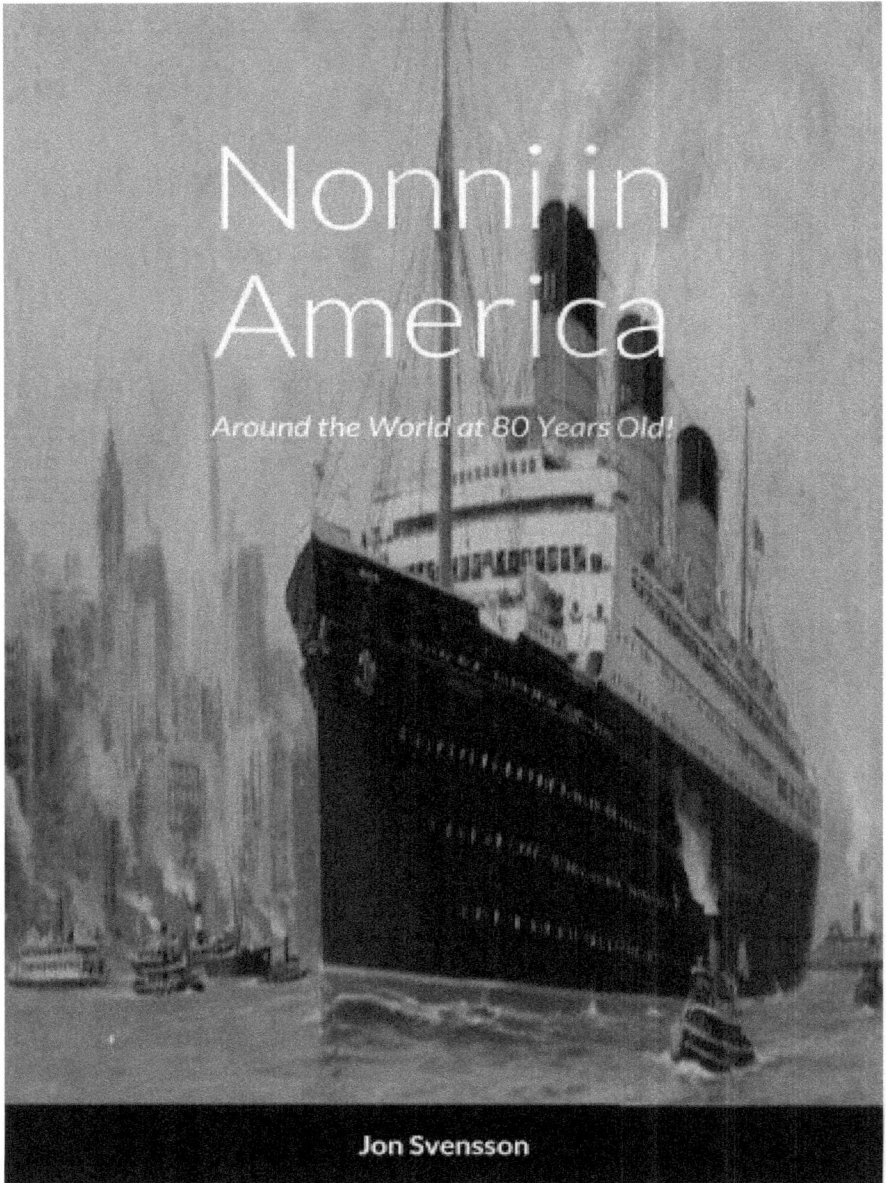

Nonni in America

Around the World at 80 Years Old!

Jon Svensson

NONNI IN AMERICA
Around the World at 80 Years Old!
by Jon Svensson

Jon Svensson was born in Iceland and is the only Jesuit priest from that island at the top of the world. After a career in teaching and ministry, he became one of the world's best loved authors by writing his series of "Nonni" books. For anyone else, such a life would seem full yet, even at age 80, he still held in his heart a boyhood dream to travel around the world and meet all of God's people. Here, for the first time in English, is the incredible true story that proves that life does not end, but really begins, at 80! "Nonni in America" features encounters with historical figures like Jules Verne, Thomas Cook, and James Garfield. It also has great descriptions of early air passenger flight, the great passenger steam ships, and the golden age of train travel. Beyond the history, "Nonni in America" has much to offer to the reader of today. For in an age when America seems to be suffering from a certain lack of confidence, Svensson takes us back to a time when American greatness was imbued in the generosity and pride of her people (large print). Now you can complete the journey by reading "Nonni in Japan."

JON SVENSSON

NONNI IN JAPAN

NONNI IN JAPAN
Around the World at 80 Years Old!

Jon Svensson was born in Iceland and is the only Jesuit priest from that island at the top of the world. After a career in teaching and ministry, he became one of the world's best loved authors by writing his series of "Nonni" books. For anyone else, such a life would seem full yet, even at age 80, he still held in his heart a boyhood dream to travel around the world and meet all of God's people. Here, for the first time in English, is the incredible true story that proves that life does not end, but really begins, at 80! "Nonni in Japan" features the second part of the great Icelandic children's writer Jon Svensson's journey around the world first begun in "Nonni in America." It is a charming and informative read which also examines the deeper topics of America and Japan on the eve of war amidst Nonni's journey of peace and understanding. Jon Svensson was fulfilling a lifelong dream to visit Japan and bring a message of peace and understanding that was very much wrapped up in his own vocation which began with an admiration of the great Jesuit missionary to Japan Saint Francis Xavier. No matter how interesting the deeper drama, one must always remember that Jon Svensson was one of the most popular writers of his day because of his great descriptive talents and storytelling abilities which are on full display here. (large print with rare period photos of the actual journey).

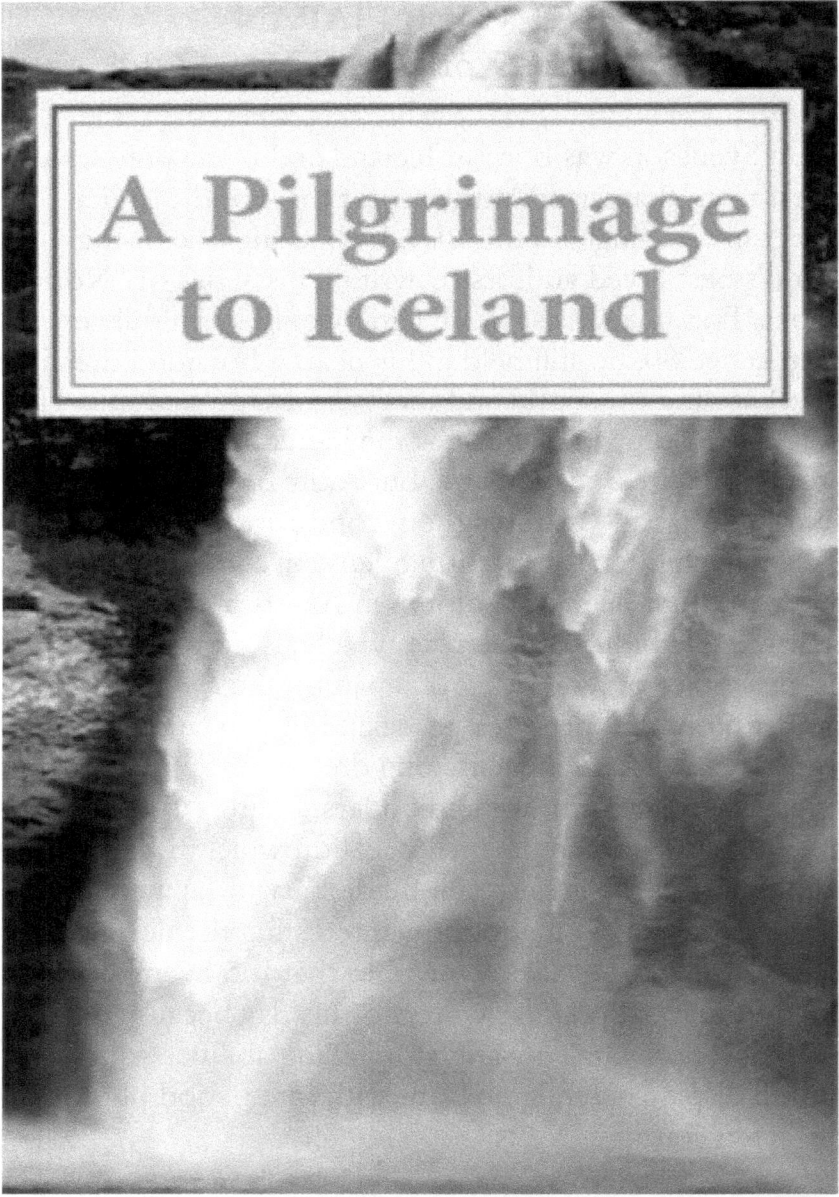

A Pilgrimage
to Iceland

A PILGRIMAGE TO ICELAND

by John C. Wilhelmsson

After the sudden loss of his father a son recalls a trip they had planned to make together. A trip to his father's homeland of Iceland some fifty years after he had left immigrated. In his grief the son decides to set out upon the journey alone in order to honor his father's memory. To set out upon a pilgrimage to Iceland. This true story features many photos. A unique combination of personal, philosophical, and spiritual reflections this book's sense of immediacy and wonder seeks to literally bring the reader along on the adventure, while its sense of reverence for the Icelandic culture, land, and people sets it apart from other tales of Iceland. This is Iceland as seen both through the mind and through the heart (large print).

Thorlak of Iceland

Who Rose Above Autism to Become Patron Saint of His People

Researched and written
by Aimee O'Connell

Thorlak of Iceland

Who Rose Above Autism to Become Patron Saint of His People

Written by Aimee O'Connell
Illustrated by Sigurbjorg Eyjolfsdottir
Foreword by John C. Wilhelmsson

Iceland's history is told in the stories of its celebrated figures. From Viking explorers to Saga heroes, the voices which define Icelandic culture are well known. Yet one man in Iceland's past had difficulty finding the words to form his own voice and be known for who he really was: Thorlák Thórhallsson, was declared "The Patron Saint of Iceland" in 1198 and officially canonized by Pope John Paul II in 1984. Yet, despite these honors, few have ever heard Thorlák's complete story: A child prodigy treated as an adult by those around him, a sorrowful boy from a broken home, a scholar of the emerging theology of merciful love, an innovator in pastoral leadership, and a man who understood the fundamental need to love and be loved. Thorlák of Iceland is an opportunity at last to celebrate this quiet hero who embodies the spiritual heart of the Icelandic people, and to learn from his inspiring true story wisdom for our own age (large print).

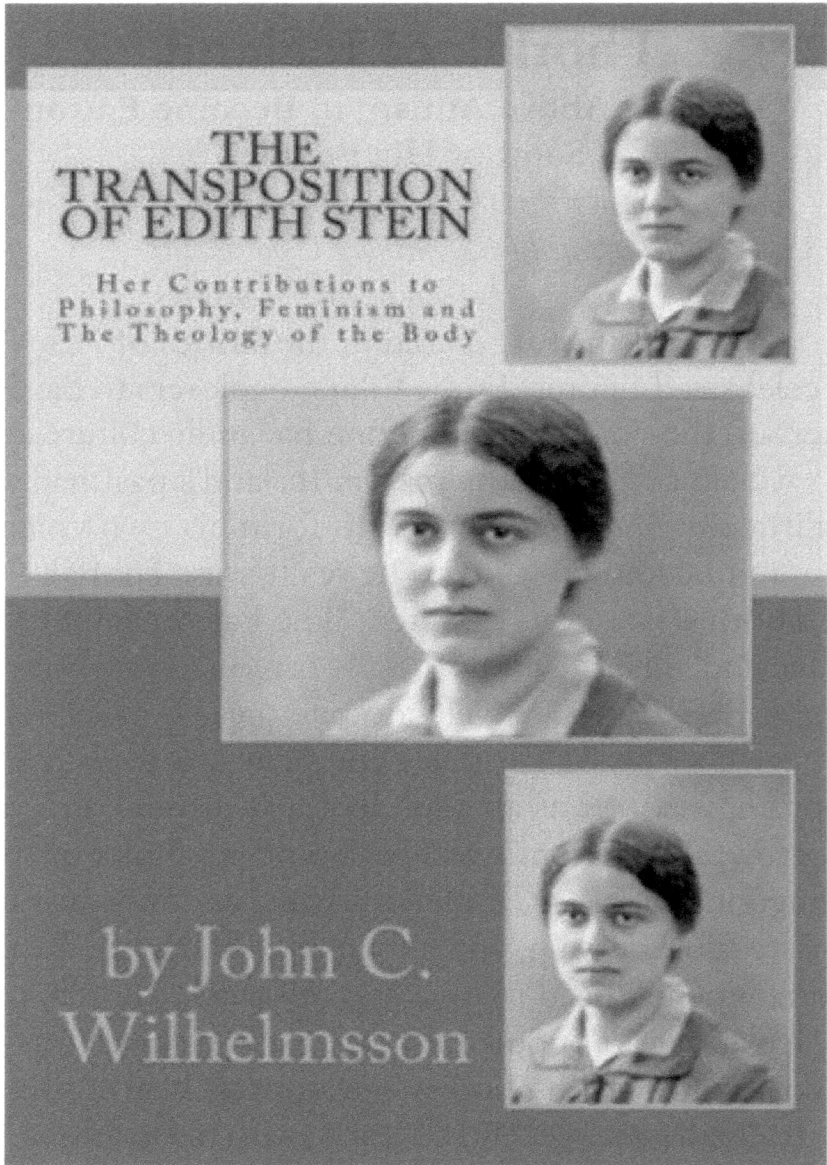

THE TRANSPOSITION OF EDITH STEIN

Her Contributions to Philosophy, Feminism, & The Theology of the Body.

by John C. Wilhelmsson

Before she was a saint she was a fine philosopher. Yet because she was a woman her contributions were ignored. This book asks the question: "Did Edith Stein make any important contributions to philosophy and, if so, what are the implications of them for us today?" It begins with a biography of Stein up until the acceptance of her doctoral dissertation "On the Problem of Empathy" in 1916. It then examines the phenomenology of Stein and, in exciting new research, demonstrates her contributions to 20th century philosophy as a whole. Finally, it looks at the feminist thought of Stein and its connection to "The Theology of the Body" of Pope John Paul II. Based upon an award winning thesis, here is a book that finally goes beyond just looking at Stein's thought as a curiosity and, instead, makes a strong argument for her contributions to philosophy, feminism, and "The Theology of the Body" (large print).

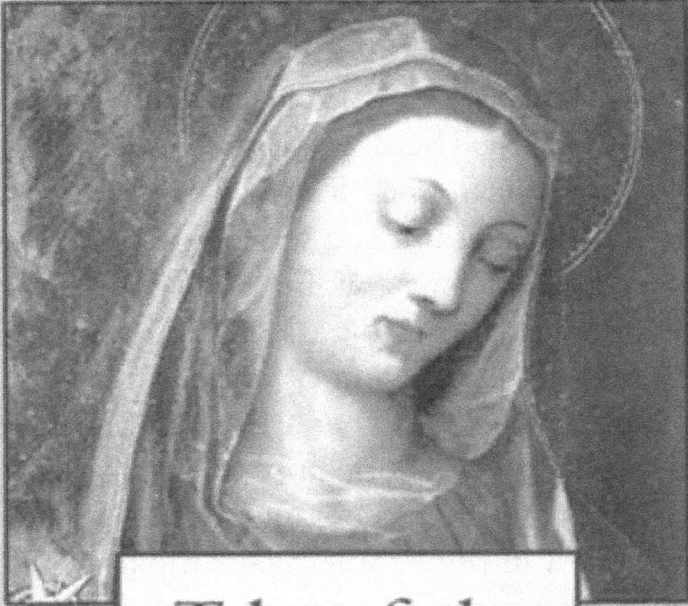

Tales of the
Theotokos

MARY IN THE PERSONAL, HISTORICAL,
SCRIPTURAL, AND SPIRITUAL REALMS.

TALES OF THE THEOTOKOS
Mary in the Personal, Historical, Scriptural, & Spiritual Realms.
by John C. Wilhelmsson

Mary is the most misunderstood figure in the history and current practice of Christianity. This book clarifies her nature and role by looking at four perspectives. "The Personal" tells of Our Lady of Guadalupe's intercession in the short story "Twin Fates." "The Historical" looks at the origins of the Rosary and Mary's influence down through the Christian age. "The Scriptural" examines Cardinal Newman's writings on Mary's role purely in terms of the Bible. And "The Spiritual" details Mary's role as Coredemptrix and the perennial truths of the spiritual life this role points to for us all. By having all of these perspectives in one unique book, "Tales of the Theotokos" takes a fresh new look at Mary the Mother of Jesus Christ (large print).

FAITH, REASON, AND THE NEW MASS TRANSLATION.

by John C. Wilhelmsson

FAITH, REASON, AND
THE NEW MASS TRANSLATION
by John C. Wilhelmsson

In late 2011 the Catholic Mass was changed from the modern English of the Novus Ordo Mass to an obtuse literal translation from Latin. According to the Catholic principle "Lex Orandi, Lex Credendi" this change in the prayer of the Church also brought with it a change in the belief of the Church. This book details the translation change and the effect it is having on Catholic belief. It also delves into the history of the issue and what the agenda behind the change really was. Featuring, "The Old 'We Believe' Crowd," "A Tale of Two Traditions," and the basic ordinary text of the 1973 Novus Ordo Mass, here is a reflection on the Mass that has shaped the faith of the English speaking world for the past 40 years along with a vigorous argument why, according to the principles of Catholic thought itself, its demise was unjust (large print).

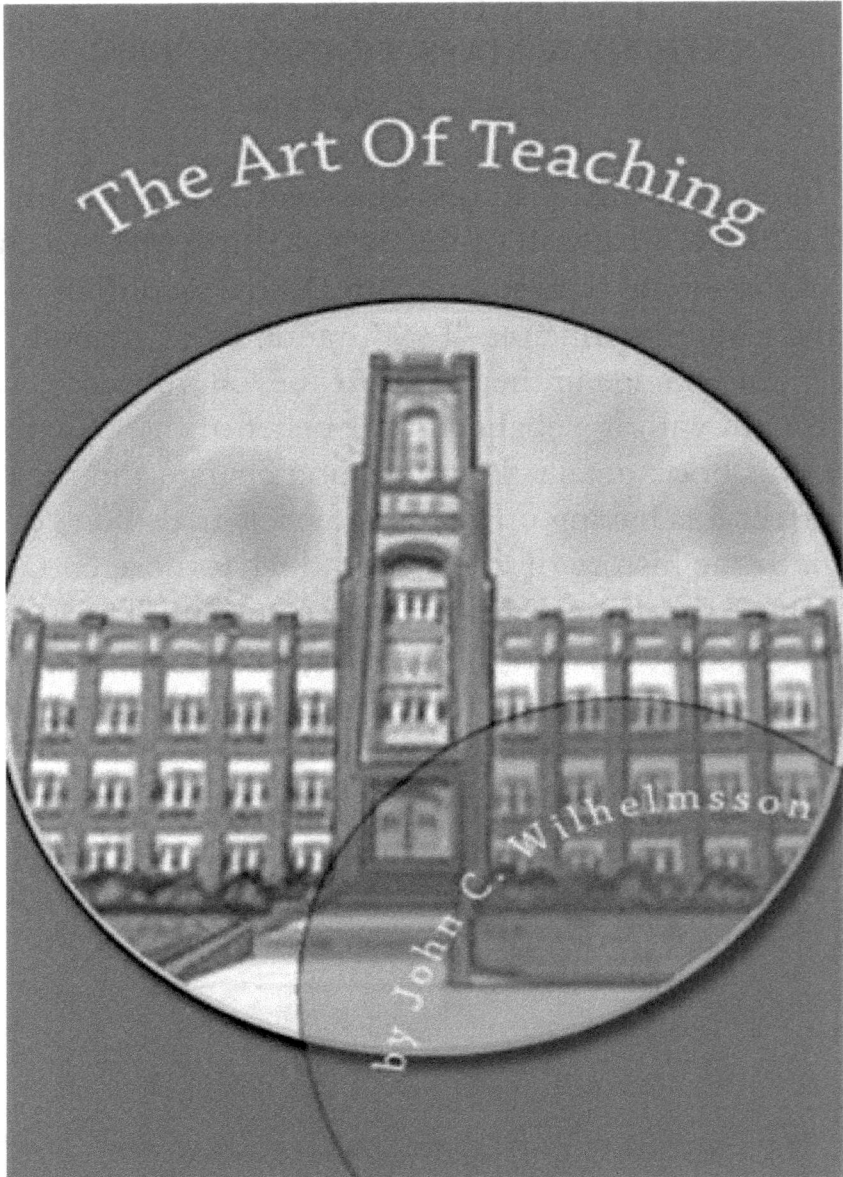

The Art Of Teaching

by John C. Wilhelmsson

THE ART OF TEACHING
AND THE THREAT OF MOOCs

by John C. Wilhelmsson

In 2013 the philosophy department at San Jose State University stood almost alone against its own administration, a group of opportunist politicians, and a well-funded high-tech start-up who were all attempting to destroy university education as we know it by pushing Massive Open Online Courses (MOOCs). In the aftermath of this modern day academic stand at Thermopylae a member of the department conducted his own reflections on the art of teaching while at the same time documenting the MOOC controversy. Here is a collection of essays on teaching born out of a real educational crisis, along with an inside perspective on the ongoing fight against MOOCs (large print).

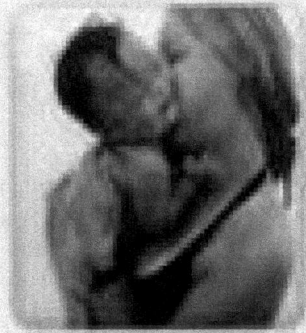

WILL ABORTION MAKE ME HAPPY?

LETTERS AND ESSAYS ON LIFE ISSUES

Will Abortion Make Me Happy?
Letters and Essays On Life Issues

by John C. Wilhelmsson

In the early twenty-first century a philosophy instructor faced with the assignment of teaching a "Moral Issues" course decided to engage in an experiment in how to teach ethics. Rather than asking whether a given issue was right or wrong he decided to ask his students whether engaging, or not engaging, in certain actions would make them happy? In doing so he was tapping in on the wisdom of classical ethics and changing the subject of such discussions from divisive arguments over competing moral codes to, what the ancients have always insisted ethics really is, a conversation about personal happiness. So begins this unique book about the abortion issue. It also features real life letters to the editor on the topic, a look at some historical aspects of the issue, and a look at how modern science has changed the way young people think about abortion (large print).

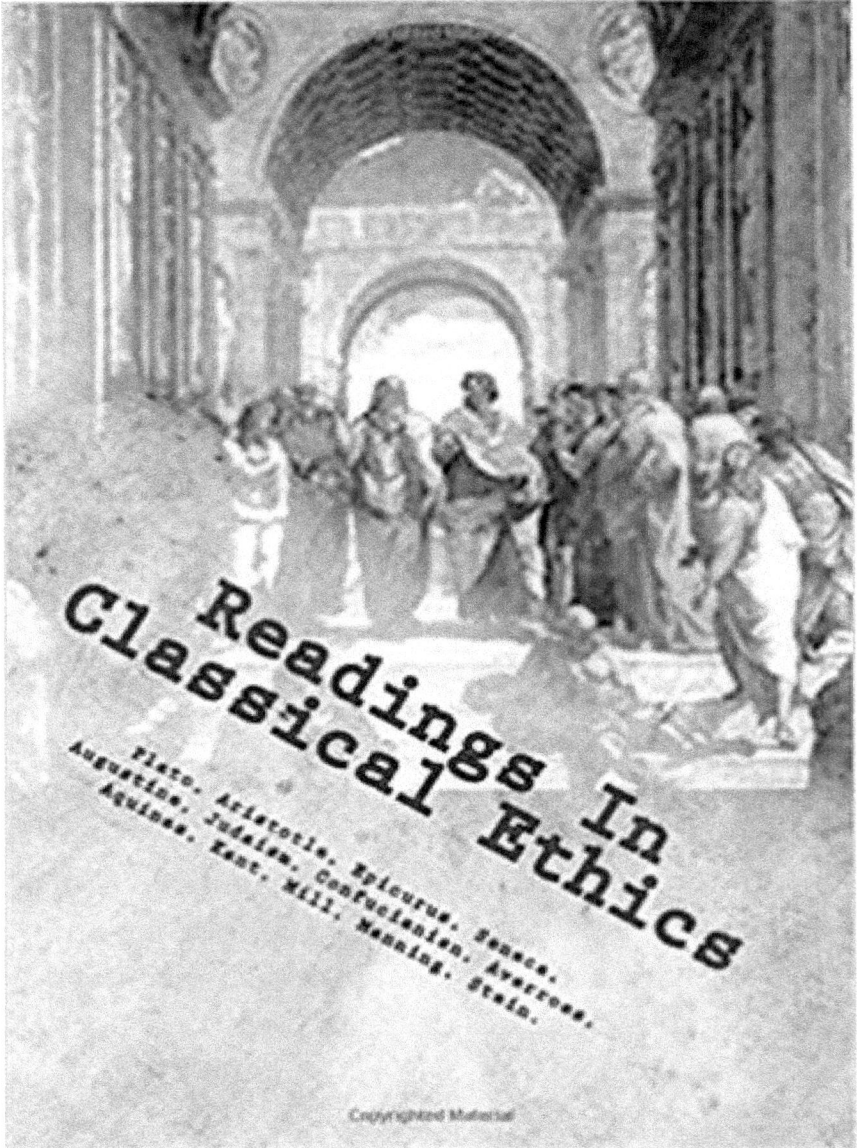

Readings In Classical Ethics
Plato, Aristotle, Epicurus, Seneca, Augustine, Kant, Mill, Manning, and Edith Stein
Edited by John C. Wilhelmsson

Readings In Classical Ethics fills the need for an Ethics reader that is easy to read because of its short selections and clear large print. Covering figures from Confucius in the 6th century BC all the way up to Edith Stein in the 20th century AD it is a comprehensive Ethics reader. Featuring selections from both Western and Eastern Philosophy, Feminist theory, Christianity, Judaism, and Islam it is a diverse Ethics reader. Published by an Ethics instructor at a reasonable price students can afford Readings In Classical Ethics is a great choice for either Ethics courses or just those with a general interest in the topic (large print).

Stoicism and its Founder

George Stock

Stoicism and its Founder

by Charles Bradlaugh and George Stock

The current fascination in Stoicism might be explained in many ways: Its insistence on being in harmony with Nature might appeal to the many young people today worried about man's relationship to the earth. Its call for discernment might appeal to those of a religious mindset seeking their calling or place in the world. Its promise of a life of meaning and peace even in the midst of chaos might appeal to the person who sees in the world today an analogy to the late the Roman Empire. Whatever the case, by combining Bradlaugh's fine essay on the founder of Stoicism Zeno along with Stock's work on Stoicism as a whole the reader can now find, in one volume, an excellent introduction to this most enduringly fascinating way of thought and life (large print).

Seven Great Freethinking Philosophers

by C. Bradlaugh
& J. Wilhelmsson

Seven Great Freethinking Philosophers
Zeno, Epicurus, Augustine, Averroes,
Descartes, Spinoza, and Edith Stein
Edited by John C. Wilhelmsson

In an age of conformity brought on by huge cult-like corporations and ubiquitous social media is there still a road less traveled one might choose? How better to confront the conformity of the 21st century than by consulting history's seven great freethinking philosophers! We live in a time of stereotypical ignorance: "Christians have narrow minds and oppose diversity;" "Muslims value blind faith over reason;" and "Women have never made any great contributions to philosophy." This book crushes these myths by detailing how seven great thinkers fought against conformity in their own ages and left us an inheritance of thought, now almost forgotten, fundamental to human dignity, the scientific method, healthy living, and academic and religious freedom. A must read for all current, or aspiring, freethinkers (large print).

www.ingramcontent.com/pod-product-compliance
Lightning Source LLC
Chambersburg PA
CBHW071347090426
42738CB00012B/3041